MW01530390

Effective Agile

AN EMPIRICAL APPROACH TO PURSUE BETTER BUSINESS OUTCOMES

SANJAY KUMAR

© *Sanjay Kumar* | *http://HowtoAgile.com*

© Sanjay Kumar | http://HowtoAgile.com

Contents

Introduction

This book is based on the core belief that "Process must subordinate to business outcomes, and not the other way around." This means that your process must enable better business outcomes and if it does not, you must be ready to alter it, evolve it or – in some cases – replace it. On the contrary, compromising business outcomes to ensure process compliance (per management order) is not only a ridiculous idea, it is against the core idea of Agile itself.

This book attempts to clarify the meaning of Agile and the 'why' behind the core disciplines of Agile. The ideas in this book are based on my readings, experience and evidences I have gathered over the past two decades as an IT professional and an Agile practitioner.

Who is this book for?

This book is written for leaders who have the responsibility of adopting Agile at team and/or organization level, which includes team leads, middle management and senior leaders. It assumes the reader has a basic understanding of Agile, through self-reading or a formal training. Some experience with Agile would certainly help though it is not an absolute must.

If this is your first book on Agile or you are a team member with less than five years of industry experience, please be warned that you may struggle with some advanced concepts.

How this book is structured?

If you talk to any two Agile practitioners, chances are you will find significant differences in their understanding of what Agile is. In the first chapter 'What is Agile?', we try to clear the air around what Agile is and what it is not. We also visit some of the common myths about Agile.

In the second chapter 'Why Agile?', we try to understand what makes Agile relevant for the knowledge work industry and discuss common benefits that could be expected from an Agile adoption – both for the customer and for the organization.

'Getting Ready for Agile' (chapter 3) serves as a transition point – where one leaves their baggage of traditional mindset and project management practices and gets ready for 'being' Agile. It is especially important for leaders in the middle/senior management that have gained expertise in traditional management practices and are now tasked with adopting Agile for their teams, business unit or organization.

In chapter 'How to be Agile?', we explore the core Agile work discipline in a framework-agnostic manner. We highlight the key Agile practices that help a team transition towards high performance culture and consistently deliver better business outcomes. A good understanding of this chapter should also help Agile leaders combine elements from different Agile frameworks or invest new Agile practices of their own.

The next chapter 'Essence of Scrum Framework' provides a brief introduction of Scrum followed by its key strengths, common implementation challenges, dysfunctions and some tips on how to succeed with your Scrum implementation. To make the best use of this chapter, prior knowledge of Scrum is highly recommended. The latest version of Scrum Guide (only about 20 pages) is a good place to start.

If you have not done any prior reading or training on Kanban Method, the last chapter 'Essence of Kanban Method' could throw some surprizes at you – because most Agile practitioners (including expert Agile coaches) carry a fairly limited understanding of Kanban. This chapter aims to deepen your understanding of Kanban and further reading (book by David Anderson) is highly recommended.

In the end, the Appendix includes few additional topics that address some common concerns among Agile practitioners but could not find a suitable place in the book elsewhere.

A final note – this is a short book that aims to refine your current understanding of Agile by filling in some important gaps that may not be covered by the books or trainings you have gone through. It will help you restructure your understanding of Agile by shattering some myths, giving new insights and providing guidance for your Agile journey, but it may not serve as a detailed step by step guide to implement a specific Agile framework.

Happy reading!

Sanjay Kumar

Email: Sanjay@HowtoAgile.com

http://HowtoAgile.com

http://LinkedIn.com/in/SunjayKumar

Acknowledgements

I consider myself fortunate that my agile journey over the past ten years has been enriching, eventful and rewarding – thanks to all the people who have helped me gain a deeper understanding of Agile mindset and practices. Below is a short list of people who stand out in their contribution to my Agile learnings and this book.

I thank my first Agile Coach, Mike Stocks, who mentored me as a Scrum Master and helped me get a good grip on Agile. It is often difficult to find Agile Coaches that focus not only on 'how' but also 'why'.

My sincere thanks to David Anderson, my teacher for Kanban Method. David is a great teacher and has helped me broaden my perspective on both Agile and coaching.

I thank Saket Bansal, the owner of iZenBridge Consultancy, for his kindness in giving me multiple training opportunities that have allowed me to share and validate my Agile knowledge with more than a thousand Agile practitioners over the past four years.

My heartfelt gratitude goes out to Tathagat Verma, Vipul Chandra, Vivek Ganesan, Rakesh Kondvilkar – reviewers for this book – who took out time from their busy schedule and shared their honest and detailed feedback. Their feedback has helped me polish the content and develop faith in the utility of this book.

I thank all my training participants over the past four years who have shared their practical agile challenges that forced me dig a little deeper and stretch my thinking on Agile.

In the end, my sincere thanks to you (the readers), who have shown faith in this book and are currently holding the book in your hands. I look forward to your honest feedback and ideas for future work.

1. What is Agile?

Agile is a simple English word but is often overloaded with meaning in the IT industry. So, lets first clear the air around what Agile is, and what it is not.

The Agile Manifesto

Seventeen people met in February 2001, at The Lodge at Snowbird ski resort in the Wasatch mountains of Utah, to talk, ski, eat, drink, relax, and - most importantly - try to find common ground for best practices for developing software. These people were experts in different processes such as Extreme Programming, Scrum, DSDM (Dynamic Systems Development Method), Adaptive Software Development, Crystal, Feature-Driven Development, Pragmatic Programming, and others. These processes collectively represented an alternate light-weight approach to the more common approach at that time – Waterfall – a process that is planning based, documentation heavy, slow to react and often relies on command and control approach to people management.

What emerged from this effort was a Manifesto for Agile Software Development, signed by all participants. The Agile Manifesto was mostly a symbolic agreement on values and principles - not a concrete process that could be straightaway adopted by a new software development team.

Here is the exact wording of the values outlined in the Agile Manifesto:

Manifesto for Agile Software Development

We are uncovering better ways of developing software by doing it and helping others do it.

Through this work we have come to value:

Individuals and interactions over processes and tools

Working software over comprehensive documentation

Customer collaboration over contract negotiation

Responding to change over following a plan

That is, while there is value in the items on the right, **we value the items on the left more.**

Principles behind the Agile Manifesto

The four values in the manifesto are accompanied by twelve principles that throw some light on the "how" of Agile:

1. Our highest priority is **to satisfy the customer** through early and continuous delivery of valuable software.
2. **Welcome changing requirements**, even late in development. Agile processes harness change for the customer's competitive advantage.
3. **Deliver working software frequently**, from a couple of weeks to a couple of months, with a preference to the shorter timescale.

4. **Business people and developers must work together daily** throughout the project.

5. Build projects around **motivated individuals**. Give them the environment and support they need, and **trust them to get the job done.**

6. The most efficient and effective method of conveying information to and within a development team is **face-to-face conversation.**

7. **Working software** is the primary measure of progress.

8. Agile processes promote **sustainable development**. The sponsors, developers, and users should be able to maintain a constant pace indefinitely.

9. **Continuous attention to technical excellence** and good design enhances agility.

10. **Simplicity** - the art of maximizing the amount of work not done - is essential.

11. The best **architectures, requirements, and designs emerge** from self-organizing teams.

12. At regular intervals, the **team reflects on how to become more effective**, then tunes and adjusts its behaviour accordingly.

Is Agile a Process or a Methodology?

A common question, often debated in Agile community, is – *Is Agile a process, framework or a Methodology?*

Before we answer this, let us try to understand these different terms:

Process: A process is a *'well defined'* set of steps and decision points for executing a specific work. Generally speaking, processes are highly repeatable, but may require occasional human intervention.

Framework: Frameworks, by definition, are a little loose. They provide structure and guidelines (against detailed or rigid instructions) on a preferred way to do a certain kind of work. They are powerful as they provide useful guidance while being flexible enough to be adapted to changing conditions, and thus can be customized for different kind of projects, organizations or industries. They usually come with multiple example implementations.

Methodology: A methodology is a detailed set of guidelines to solve a specific problem, and usually comes with a defined set of rules, practices, methods, testing approach and metrics. Methodologies demonstrate a well thought out, repeatable approach – more detailed and stricter than a process.

To put things in Agile perspective, Extreme Programming (XP) is a methodology and Scrum could be called a process or a process framework depending on how strictly it is being implemented. For example, you may call 'ritualistic Scrum' a process where a coach enforces Scrum implementation strictly by the book (a book of their choice).

What about Agile?

While we hear the phrase 'Agile process' and 'Agile methodology' in common parlance, it is none as the Agile manifesto does not provide enough guidance on how to get started with an Agile implementation. It provides useful work discipline but not specific practices to be followed. It is silent on details like – should we use iterations, what roles should we have, what meetings, or how to manage requirements. Agile manifesto provides a 'way of thinking' more than a way of doing things. This is the primary reason that most Agile experts like to call Agile a 'mindset', rather than a process or a methodology.

Common Myths/Misconceptions about Agile

Agile = Scrum

Agile is a thought process, a collection of values and principles. There are different ways of being Agile as a team – Scrum being the most popular, most widely adopted way of starting the Agile journey. Assuming Agile is equal to Scrum is an incorrect understanding that could sometimes prove to be a costly mistake. Some other ways to adopt Agile include Kanban Method and Extreme Programming. And yes, you could also embrace practices from these three frameworks and create your own Agile process.

Agile mandates iterations

Agile manifesto talks about 'early and continuous delivery' (principle #1) and 'preference to the shorter timescale' (principle #3), but it does not mandate developing solutions in fixed timeboxed iterations. It is up to the team to practice iterative batch flow or continuous flow of work.

Please refer chapter 'Essence of Kanban Method' to explore how a team could practice agility using continuous flow (without a strict timebox).

Agile is easy, all you need is...

There are different versions of this statement, mostly by leaders who have gained theoretical knowledge on Agile (through book or training) but are yet to see and experience how agile really works. Their thinking is – you just need to change the process/structure, and everything else will follow.

The idea of Agile could be simple, but it requires a lot of self-discipline (by all involved) and takes a long learning curve.

Agile means no documentation

Primarily an incorrect understanding of second value statement in the manifesto, it is commonly used by developers as an excuse not to document anything. To be clear, Agile does not suggest 'no documentation'. It suggests we focus more on creating solution rather than detailed documentation that is more of a compliance requirement and rarely kept up-to-date or referred to in future. Optimal documentation that will be referred to for future decision making is still a great idea.

Agile means no planning

A statement mostly used by someone who lacks self-discipline and works in a reactive mode rather than a proactive manner. It could be a Product Owner, a new Scrum Master (erstwhile Manager who likes to work in a fire-fighting mode) or team members who like to work at their own pace.

The right statement is 'Agile uses adaptive planning'. More details to follow in chapter 'Key Agile Practices'.

Agile is for software development only

Right, Agile manifesto was written as a guidance for software development; there are multiple references to the word 'software'. But, since then, encouraged by the success of Agile in software development, organizations have adopted Agile as new ways of working (NWOW) in other domains such as HR, marketing, R&D and other non-IT projects.

While Agile was meant for software development, saying it is **only** for software development would be a close-minded thought. In the manifesto, if we change the word 'software' to 'solution' (product or service), it starts making much better sense – and for all domains, not just IT.

Please review 'Revisiting the Agile Manifesto' in Appendix for a newer, industry-neutral version of the manifesto.

2. Why Agile: The Value Proposition

No one should adopt Agile, or any other approach, just because everyone else seems to be following it. Treating Agile like fashion could be a costly mistake. Sometimes, very very costly. Change must be relevant and beneficial to be meaningful. Otherwise, it is just a fad or a vanity statement.

The benefits from Agile can be broadly categorized into two sections – benefits for the business/customer, and benefits for the management or service organization:

Benefits to the Business/Customer

1. **Value-driven delivery:** Team collaborates with business/customer to build what really matters, leading to better product alignment with market needs.
2. **Faster time to market (or faster ROI):** Products features are built and deployed every few days/weeks rather than only once in several months.
3. **Better transparency of work progress:** Customers get to real time progress of how their money is being spent, plus they get to view the working software on a frequent basis.
4. **Responsiveness to change:** Agile teams are open to changes in requirements (not always free though) whether they are due to changing market dynamics or improved understanding of the product.

5. **Predictability of work completion:** Agile teams often exhibit a more predictable pace, both in terms of how much (velocity/throughput) and how fast (cycle time) items are completed once committed.

Benefits to the Organization

1. **High Customer Satisfaction:** Agile teams collaborate with the customer regularly thereby spending their effort in alignment with market needs, leading to higher customer satisfaction.

2. **Sustainable and predictable pace of development:** Agile teams are empowered and supported to make their own decisions (executional, not strategic), resulting in less reliance on external factors and achieving a more predictable pace of work progress.

3. **Continuously evolving process:** Agile teams reflect on their process and make an attempt to enhance it regularly.

4. **Reduced process waste:** A result of value-driven delivery and continuously evolving process.

5. **Motivated work environment (low attrition rate):** Empowered Agile teams that have learned to self-manage their work enjoy higher levels of individual confidence, technical ability and overall work satisfaction.

What makes Agile work?

Yes, Agile works!

The period of doubt, confusion and resistance in the IT industry is pretty much history now. The success of Agile is visible and widespread, with enough successful case studies out there. We have reached a stage where if an IT organization (or department) is not using Agile methods already, it certainly wants to – and may often experience extreme guilt for delaying it any further.

But we should not go by the direction of the wind, instead must try logical reasoning to understand if Agile makes sense. Let us go through some important concepts in order to answer the question "Why Agile makes sense?"

Defined Work vs Knowledge Work

Broadly speaking, the professional work humans do can be categorized into two types – defined work and knowledge work. Defined work is repetitive work that usually becomes quite predictable (throughput and cycle time) with time. Here are some examples:

- o Fast food menu items
- o Chairs (standard design) made by a carpenter
- o Painting of a house by a professional team
- o An experienced clerk typing X number of pages on a typewriter or computer

Knowledge work on the other hand, involves more thinking time. While there are success patterns in knowledge work, it may not follow a standard path – leading to higher variation in throughput (how much) and cycle time (how fast). Here are some examples:

- o An artist making a new scenery or a portrait (not a repeat)
- o A writer writing a new poem or song
- o A student preparing for an exam
- o A nanny trying to calm a crying child
- o A software developer writing new code

Stacey Matrix

Developed by Ralph D. Stacey, the Stacey matrix provides a method to select an appropriate management action in a complex adaptive system based on the degree of certainty and level of agreement.

Adapted for knowledge work projects, it may roughly translate to technology on the horizontal axis and requirements on the vertical axis. As you can see in the picture, it divides the entire space into four areas:

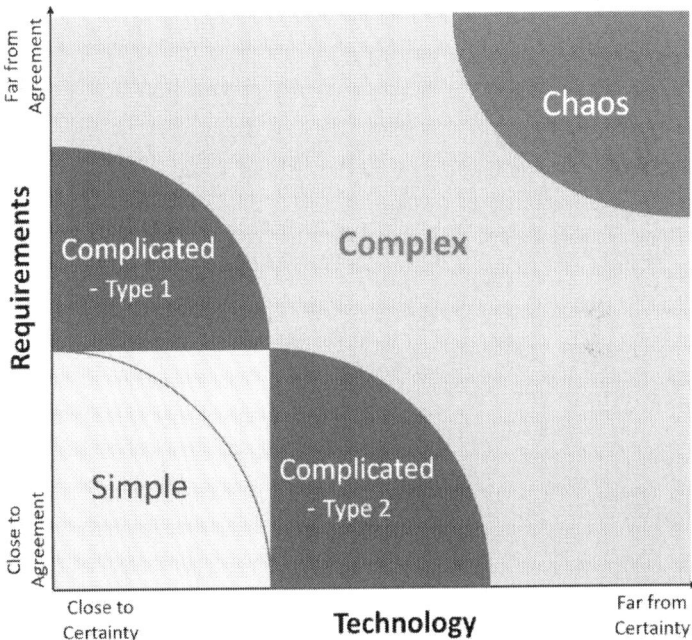

Simple Decision Making: Requirements close to agreement and technical approach close to certainty. History provides accurate guidance – planning relies on using data from the past to predict future outcomes with minimal variance. Here, waterfall-like big upfront planning approach may work perfectly well. A website design project using one of the available Wordpress themes could be an example of this.

Complicated Decision Making – Type 1: Here, the technical approach is well established, but requirements are expected to evolve with time. In other words, we know how to achieve outcomes, but not clear on what outcomes to achieve. One example could be a website design with lot of custom static content but limited user interaction – like a corporate website.

Complicated Decision Making – Type 2: There is good agreement on requirements, but things need to be explored on the technology front. Think of banking automation projects in the eighties and nineties where most banks automated their internal operations – replacing their old manual record-keeping practices. A recent example could be a bank building mobile application for their retail customers, with the mobile app functionality expected to be a subset of existing banking website.

Complex Decision Making: There is fair agreement on requirement and good enough understanding on technical approach, but overall more is unknown than is known. A bank building its first mobile application could be one good example, especially when some other banks have already launched their mobile application and the team has developers who have done mobile app development before. So, we have some idea on both requirements and technical approach, but both are expected to evolve significantly during development.

Chaotic Decision Making: This is a case of high uncertainty on both fronts – requirements and technology. Think of the first bank who decided to launch their mobile app and assume that they did not have a team with experience in mobile app development. Instead, they expected the existing web app development team to learn mobile app development while building it. Here we have a chaotic environment, with lot of going back and forth on requirements as well as technical approach – an extremely uncertain environment possibly with high level of stress.

Given the inherent uncertainty in Complicated, Complex and Chaotic work, would it be wise to indulge in heavy upfront planning and expect the project to go exactly as planned?

Definitely not. Unfortunately, that is what companies tried to do for several decades in the name of Waterfall process. While it gave them (and clients) pseudo confidence of being on track and successful for the big initial part of the project, the reality eventually caught up with them – most waterfall projects were delivered late, and some had to be scrapped with a lot of 'sunk cost'.

Stress vs Performance

A quick exercise before we proceed.

Please think for a moment – what is the relationship between stress and performance? How does individual performance change as the stress level goes up? You may draw a chart with stress on the X-axis and performance on the Y-axis (see blank graph below).

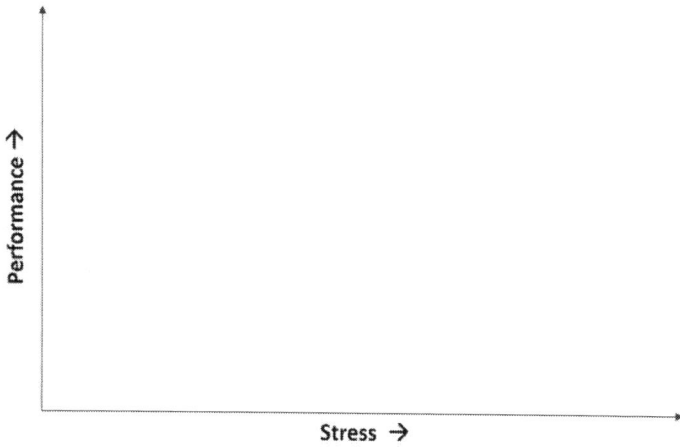

The shape of Stress vs. Performance curve would depend a lot on an individual's personality – as different people respond to stress in different ways. For most people, the performance would go through following three phases as stress goes up:

Complacency

This is the phase of low energy levels and low performance, where people are mostly inactive, bored and/or under-committed. Some common examples could be clerical staff in most government offices, most offices in holiday season towards the end of the year, and first few months in a waterfall project.

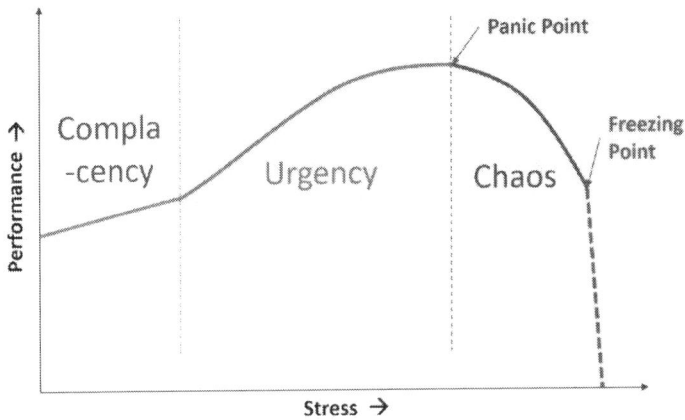

Urgency

As the stress level crosses a threshold, sense of urgency sets in leading to improved performance. This is the phase of healthy stress that improves focus and commitment. As stress increases, the performance continues to improve until it reaches a peak, which will very likely be different for different individuals.

The most common trigger is an approaching deadline for an item or the entire release – say, when a waterfall project approaches QA cycle. Managers have long known this positive impact of an approaching deadline and thus usually prefer having a deadline on each individual item.

Chaos

If we continue to increase stress beyond the peak performance level, it sets in panic leading to a negative impact on performance. This Chaos phase is what gives people heartburn, makes people sweat, their hands begin to shake, and their words follow an incoherent rhythm. A high stress situation is unhealthy for the individual and the organization. Besides inconsistent productivity, it usually leads to poor quality.

A common example is the last month of a waterfall project where the rush of getting the project done forces quality to take a backseat. There are many examples in everyday life where extremely high demand may increase stress levels to unhealthy levels – weekend dinner at famous restaurants, holiday shopping season (Thanksgiving Sale!) in malls, etc.

The Essence of Agile

Back to the original question – what makes Agile work?

Keeping in mind the concepts we just discussed, we need an approach that:

1. Can handle the uncertainty associated with knowledge work:
   - Can adapt to changes in requirements
   - Can adapt to uncertainty in technical approach
2. Helps team work with a sense of Urgency, minimizing the periods of Complacency and Chaos

Unlike Waterfall, Agile embraces reality – the uncertainty associated with knowledge work – and takes an adaptive approach that has deep roots in empiricism.

Below is a high level summary of Agile approach. For a detailed list of Agile practices, please see chapter 'Key Agile Practices'.

1. Incremental Development & Delivery

Agile focuses on achieving the outcome (say, product development) in an incremental manner. Rather than finishing the entire project in one shot, an Agile team focuses on finishing small features/functionality on a regular basis. For a Scrum team, the idea of a Sprint (2 weeks to 1 month) provides a useful structure that promotes incremental development. A Kanban team uses a continuous item-based flow (rather than a batch-flow) to practice incremental development.

The practice of incremental development minimizes the risks associated with uncertain requirements/technology by committing to a small set of requirements, producing evidence of success, learning from it and refining the approach for the next set of requirements. It enables the team to use an adaptive approach to problem solving and value creation.

Waterfall Process

An Agile Process (iteration based)

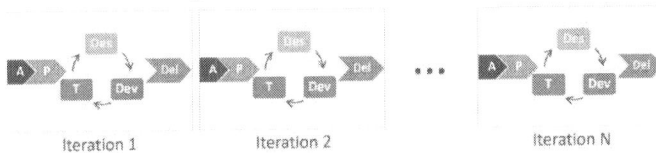

A key enabler for incremental development is the practice of 'faster feedback cycle' that encourages team to get feedback from testers, PO, UAT team and stakeholders on a regular basis and within hours/days rather than after weeks/months.

These smaller cycles of work completion along with 'faster feedback cycle' bring in a sense of urgency and help prevent the Chaos phase towards the end of the project that is often caused by big batch of UAT or customer feedback.

2. Continuous Improvement

While incremental development helps minimize the risk, the practice of continuous improvement ensures teams progressively build knowledge by learning from past results and refine their approach through frequent 'inspect and adapt' cycles. Besides minimizing risk and cost, it also provides an opportunity for individual and team growth.

3. Self-organizing culture

In an Agile environment, it is the team that collectively owns the work (code) and takes the executional responsibility for delivery. The work-related decision making is also de-centralized, with team practicing participatory decision making that builds on collective intelligence of the entire team rather than a few experts.

A word of caution – it is extremely important that to enable the team, the team lead (whatever be the title) must give up the 'leading from the front' style and must adopt the path of facilitative leadership. It is usually a big learning curve that is often under-estimated and poorly implemented, posing a big risk to the success of an Agile transition.

3. Getting Ready for Agile

Each organization or team transitioning to Agile is keen to achieve benefits of Agile, but not all are aware of the essential mindset needed before we start our Agile transition – often leading to a bumpy transition ride that is rife with confusion and resistance. In this chapter, we look at two foundational elements that need the attention of leadership – the mindset shifts required and a new comprehensive way to look at team capability.

Mindset Shift required for Agile Leadership

In most cases, the Agile transition is approved and often championed by the senior management. While the leaders are convinced about the benefits of Agile, they often understand it to be a change that impacts only the teams. I have often seen Agile practitioners complain: "management wants us to completely change our ways of thinking and doing things, but they don't want to change an inch themselves." Thinking Agile transition is a localized change (at team level) is a big misunderstanding that could severely limit the potential of the entire organization.

If an organization really wants to sustain and scale the benefits of Agile, they must embrace the Agile mindset at all levels. That is right, the leadership team also needs to adopt an Agile mindset, and in the same direction, here are five key cultural shifts that are essential:

1. Culture of taking orders -> Culture of meaningful conversations

When agile is introduced in a traditional organization where structural hierarchy is valued a lot, the self-managing culture usually takes a backseat. What you witness instead is the culture of 'taking orders' – Product Owner taking orders from the customer, Scrum Master (or team lead) taking orders from management, and the team in turn taking orders from both Product Owner and Scrum Master.

Simply instructing and expecting the teams to be self-organizing is of little use when the value of hierarchy is so pervasive in the organization. The transition to Agile would require a new culture to be promoted – the culture of 'value-driven meaningful conversations' where individuals do not simply take orders but try to understand the 'why' behind each request and show courage in asking questions (humble enquiry) when there is lack of clarity or a difference of opinion. This of course will not be a quick switch but is a slow transition that requires long term efforts especially by the people with authority.

2. Accurate Estimates -> Inherent Variability in Knowledge Work

As we discussed previously, unlike defined work, knowledge work has inherent variability which makes it difficult to estimate. In knowledge work industry the term 'accurate estimate' is an oxymoron. If a developer writes 100 lines of code on Monday, it does not mean he will continue to code that much each single day of that week and thereafter. Not to mention, all 100 lines of code do not equate to same amount of work (story points).

In my experience, the organizations and teams that focus too hard on accurate estimates usually end up with delayed plans and stressed/demotivated teams.

3. Firm and frozen plans -> Adaptive planning

Given the inherent variability in knowledge work, expecting firm release dates, with fixed or ever-changing scope is a wish that may never come true. The variability in knowledge work must be embraced, and instead of wasting time in detailed long-term planning, the lean approach of short-term adaptive planning must be chosen.

While we may no longer have firm and frozen plans (whose false certainty felt so comforting to the management), we take the path of 'continuous effort/value optimization' to ensure human effort is being spent towards what really matters.

4. Maximizing Team Productivity -> Maximizing Business Value Delivery

In the recent past, I have heard about too many instances where management has pushed down a directive on Agile teams to target X% increase in productivity (velocity) every sprint. This smells like old world thinking where the focus is on resource optimization rather than maximizing value creation and delivery. Often, such decisions are taken in a state of panic, perhaps triggered by some leader's desperate need to show some improved numbers as a proof of better returns on investment in an Agile initiative.

While the intention may be right (e.g., measure team performance and improvement), the execution idea looks severely flawed. It reflects that management has failed to understand the basic idea of sustainable pace besides failing to develop value-driven focus.

5. Planning work for the team -> Team planning their own work

An organization may decide to replace the Manager role with the Scrum Master role, but it is difficult for that person to switch quickly to a new set of behaviour. As the saying goes... 'old habits die hard'. The new Scrum Master (ex-manager) might continue to take lead in planning work for the team – purely out of habit or owing to lack of faith in team's capability. And, not just planning, they might continue to closely monitor each team member's productivity and efficiency, sometimes using metrics such as story points completed by each developer or defects raised by each tester.

Let us spend a moment here to understand the motivation behind self-organizing teams.

Imagine an organization has the need to start a new project that is expected to require a team of ten work together for about a year. If it is an organization practising traditional management, good chances are that they would look for a manager first – a person who has the required domain and/or technical expertise and has experience in leading a team of this size. Then, they would create a team of ten around the manager –something like a star-shaped structure, with manager in the centre of all decision making. Team members are expected to look up to the manager for guidance and key decision making. Nothing moves without the knowledge and approval of the manager. Of course, each team environment would be different, but would heavily depend on two primary factors – organizational culture and the personality of the Manager. That is how most industries have worked for decades.

Here are common side-effects of such a star-shaped team arrangement:

a. **Single point of failure:** Given the over-dependence on Manager, she could prove to be a single point of failure for different reasons:

   - Lack of availability – too busy with work or out on vacation.

   - Outdated expertise – she may believe herself to be a technical expert, but we all know how fast the technology changes. She may be ill-equipped to make the right decisions and no team member may have guts to tell her so.

   - A random poor decision – even as an expert, it is difficult to make right decisions all the time. And, a manager is no exception, even if she is a domain/technical expert. While some team member may see a risk with a particular poor decision, they may not feel empowered enough to raise the concern.

b. **Low Team Morale:** Among knowledge workers, 'autonomy' is one of the key intrinsic motivators. Hiring smart employees and expecting them to strictly follow orders is guaranteed to create disconnected employees with low motivation and morale, leading to poor quality, uncertain productivity and high attrition.

c. **Limited Knowledge sharing:** When people are told what to do, they don't get an opportunity to think and share their ideas. It promotes silo culture. The high performers continue to enhance their skills while others resort to a follower mindset, limiting their professional growth and potential.

Agile promotes team empowerment and self-management to remove the risks posed by a star-shaped team structure. A self-managing team practices participatory decision making where all team members participate in the decision-making process rather than take orders from the team lead. The idea is to learn from and build on collective intelligence, and not to make the team lead redundant. As shown in the picture, the team lead is still needed, not as a Manager (M) but as an enabler (E), a facilitator, a servant leader.

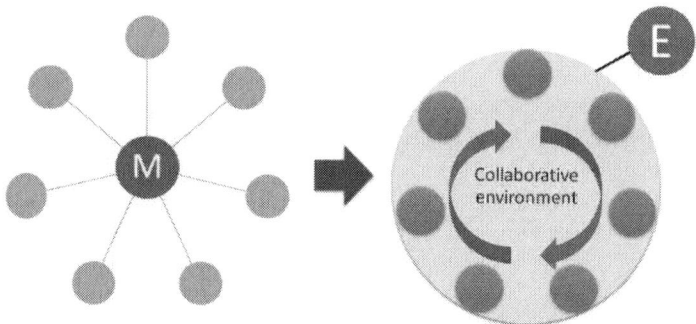

The practice of participatory decision making has several benefits:

- Decisions are more robust as they build on collective intelligence
- Creates an opportunity for team members to learn from each other
- Improves trust and respect among team members
- Decisions are more likely to be respected and followed through
- It promotes a culture of excellence and professional growth

5 Dimensions of Team Capability

How would you evaluate a team's capability? What would make you say that a team has improved its capability in the past 3 or 6 months?

Of course, Productivity is a key measure of a team's capability but too much emphasis on it (often management's obsession with it) could create a stressful and unhealthy environment.

Below I share five dimensions of team capability that I have found helpful during initial discussions with the leadership. It helps stretch their thinking beyond productivity and prepares them better for an Agile approach.

1. Productivity

This is a measure of 'how much' work a team finishes in a specified time period. For a Scrum team, you may roughly equate it to team's velocity (total number of story points completed in a Sprint). For a team practicing Kanban, it may be either be the total number of items completed per day/week/month (ignoring the difference in their size), or – if they practice relative estimation – the total number of story points completed per time period.

2. Quality

If productivity is 'how much' work was done, quality is 'how well' it was done. It refers to the craftmanship of work completion. While there are more measures for quality than productivity, there is poor consistency in how Agile teams measure quality.

Below are some common metrics for measuring quality (some more useful than others):

- Number of escaped defects – Production
- Number of escaped defects – outside team environment (UAT, System/Integration testing)
- Number of defects during development (QA)
- Code coverage (%)
- Total technical debt
- Code quality metrics

3. Turnaround Time

This is 'how fast' team finishes the committed work and has two dimensions:

a. **Item turnaround time (Cycle Time/ Lead Time):** This is how fast the team completes an item after it has been committed. Cycle Time is the total elapsed time from commitment to completion by the team, not the effort spent (person days) on the item. Lead Time goes a little further and measures elapsed time from commitment to delivery to the customer, and may include waiting times (UAT, approvals, etc.) that are outside the team's direct control.

A shorter Cycle Time is of course better, but even more important is the overall variance among Cycle time for all items in a given period. A high variance (wider range) in cycle time would indicate low predictability of work completion, and hence, lower team capability.

b. **Release Frequency:** This is how often a team releases the finished product to production environment. A team that releases to production every week is considered more Agile than a team that releases once a month, and both are more agile than a team that releases only once a quarter or six months – all other factors being the same. While there may be some environmental constraints that make it difficult to release the product more frequently, an agile team must always look for the possibility of releasing more often. The key point here is not to release more often than another team in one's own or in another organization, but to explore the possibility of releasing more often than you do now. The aim should be to shorten the cycle from Value Discovery to Value Delivery.

4. Business Value Delivery

Value delivery might sound like Productivity but there is a difference – it is not how much 'work' is completed but how much 'value' has been created (and possibly delivered) in a time period.

If a Scrum team maintains a consistent velocity of 25 story points from Sprint N to Sprint N+1, one might argue that their productivity in both sprints is the same. Sounds quite right – roughly, if not exactly. But, can one safely assume the team has created/delivered the same amount of value in both Sprints?

Probably not.

The value created would depend not only on how much work was completed but – more importantly – which specific work items were completed.

There are three key components of value-delivery:

a. **Value Discovery:** Identifying items that will (or might) deliver value to the end users and customers, and prioritize them in order of expected value delivery.

b. **Value Creation:** Doing what really matters, and among them, first do what matters the most.

c. **Value Delivery:** Deploy to production more frequently rather than only once in several months. This may require regular and timely engagement of the team with the downstream system – including but not limited to UAT team, customers and operations team.

As may be obvious, Value Discovery is a precondition for Value Creation and Value Delivery.

If you hand over a useless requirement to the team, a perfect development process can only help minimize the time wasted on that item, not deliver business value (that did not exist in the first place).

Some basics to keep in mind:

1. No process will turn 'crap' into 'gold'!
2. An ineffective product discovery process could be the biggest waste in your system as it will waste the capacity of everyone downstream.
3. In case of too many customer voices, care must be taken to balance them else it might lead to inconsistent product behaviour and quality.

5. Self-Organizing Behaviour

A team that consistently produces good quality work at good pace is great, and a team that does the same on their own (with minimal guidance) is even better. Self-organizing behaviour makes team performance more consistent and more predictable, besides building an environment of high motivation and trust. Recently, I observed a team slack a little when the team lead was on vacation. Their productivity had gone down almost 50% in those two weeks. The primary focus of a team coach in this case would be to improve team's self-organizing behaviour.

In the past one year, I have come across several organizations that had started their Agile journey 2-3 years ago, new Agile process (mostly Scrum) was brought in, team structure changed, things improved a little process-wise, but the management was not happy. Their key complaints were lack of self-organizing culture and lack of predictability in work completion – it is likely that both could be related.

Below are some of the key characteristics of a self-organizing team:

- **Cross-Functional:** To become self-organizing, it is almost essential that the team (as a whole) possesses all the skills required to produce value – to convert requirements into finished product. An important clarification here – a cross-functional team does not imply that each team member must be multi-skilled. It just means that the team members collectively possess all the skills required.
  A team that lacks required skills may end up having significant external dependencies, leading to unpredictable pace of value creation and may fail to develop the required trust among team members.
- **Alignment:** The team goals are clear and transparent and team members' efforts are targeted towards achieving the same. In other words, team goals take higher priority than individual goals.
- **Transparency:** Everyone can see how much work is where, who is working on what, how do the metrics look, what is blocked and how long, etc.

- **Empowerment:** Team is empowered for local decision making – regarding how to plan and execute their work.
- **Collaboration:** Team dynamics are collaborative and exhibit positive energy. Members approach each other on regular basis.
- **Achievement Orientation:** The team members display high commitment and accountability. They work with a sense of urgency (not complacency, stress or panic) – almost like they are addicted to doing a great job.
- **Self-Belief:** Though it might take a while to get there, a self-organizing team has strong self-belief in getting things done. This is especially useful in challenging times when an ordinary team may fall apart with individual members acting in an individualistic and self-defensive manner.

4. How to be Agile?

Value-driven focus, empiricism and self-organizing teams are the heart of Agile. Along the same lines, below are five key elements of Agile work discipline that help teams advance in their Agile journey, irrespective of their chosen framework:

    i.   Self-organizing teams

    ii.   Iterative value discovery

    iii.   Incremental value creation

    iv.   Frequent value delivery

    v.   Continuous improvement

In the rest of this chapter, we will discuss these five disciplines in detail with their specific practices.

1. Self-Organizing Teams

As mentioned in the previous chapters, agile puts a lot of emphasis on self-organization. While there are some differences in actual practices, the idea of self-organization is promoted by all agile processes. It is an enabler for team motivation and sustainable pace of development.

The key practices that foster self-organizing culture include:

1.1   Visualize Work

Visualizing work is a core practice of Kanban Method, but its use is widespread among most Agile teams. Mature Agile teams actively use visualization of work whether it is an electronic board, a physical board or both. It is a key enabler for self-organizing culture as it brings transparency among team members:

a. How much work is currently in progress?
b. How does the work flow through the system (sequence of activities)?
c. What is the current status of all committed work – how much work is where?
d. Who is working on what item?
e. Which items are blocked or held up, and for what reason?
f. What work is planned for the near future?

1.2   Participatory Decision Making

As discussed under section 'Mindset Shift required for Agile Leadership', the work-related decision making is de-centralized in Agile, with team practicing participatory decision making that builds on collective intelligence (individuals and interactions) of the entire team rather than a few experts. Good facilitation skills are a 'must-have' for the team leader in Agile context.

1.3   Team Empowerment

In an Agile environment, the team owns the work (code) and takes the executional responsibility for delivery. Coming from a traditional management, this is a big empowerment for the team and its members.

As they say, 'with power comes responsibility'. Members of a self-organizing team collaborate with each other in a timely manner. They do not wait until the next morning Daily standup, or until the team lead asks them, or until they have been stuck with a problem for several hours/days. They raise impediments, seek and share knowledge, seek help, and help others as the need arises, in a proactive manner, without any hesitance.

1.4   Team Leader as a Coach

Here the term 'team leader' refers to roles like Scrum Master (Scrum), Service Delivery Manager (Kanban Method), Agile Project Manager (Hybrid?), etc.

As the ownership of the Goal/Delivery moves to the team, the role of a team lead does not become any less important. In fact, it becomes more important and often very difficult as it requires an erstwhile manager to adopt a new mindset – the coaching mindset:

- Teams often struggle in their journey to self-organizing work culture as it requires each team member to transition from an 'I' mindset to the 'We' mindset. Team Lead plays a critical role here working as an 'enabler' for team's transition to this new culture. [Refer section 'Self-Organizing Behaviour' under '5 Dimensions of Team Capability']
- Team Lead helps create a safe team environment that is open and trustful, where team members seek help, challenge each other and hold each accountable without hesitation and without the fear of being judged.
- Team Lead acts like a Coach helping the team accomplish meaningful business results and grow as professionals in the journey.
- Team Lead acts like a Servant Leader serving the purpose of the team, rather than expecting the team to serve her purpose.

1.5   Explicit Policies (Entry/Exit Criteria)

Agile teams discuss and agree on a common work discipline that helps them optimize their efforts. And, to avoid confusion and ambiguity that might creep in with time, they write and publicize the policies that guides their work discipline.

In Scrum, teams often practice Definition of Ready (DoR) that helps teams decide if a backlog item is ready to be pulled into Sprint (entry criteria) and Definition of Done (DoD) that helps decide if an item has been completed as per expectations (exit criteria).

In Kanban Method, the explicit policies are more granular and are defined at the activity level, giving guidance on work discipline while carrying out the individual activities. The explicit policies may also be defined for classes of service to avoid ambiguity among stakeholders.

2.   Iterative Value Discovery

2.1   Progressive Elaboration

The team takes an incremental approach to understand and detail the requirements. A relevant analogy offered by Mike Cohn for the list of requirements is that of an iceberg where the tip of the iceberg represents the fine-grained requirements well understood by the team and expected to be picked up for development in the coming few weeks, while the bottom part of the iceberg represents coarsely grained requirements planned for the long term.

2.2   Regular Collaboration with Business Stakeholders

The fourth principle in Agile Manifesto reads "Business people and developers must work together daily throughout the project." The focus here is to ensure we build the "right" product. There are two common challenges here:

- There might be a disconnect in understanding of the "right" product between the business and the team, despite all the documents and conversations that happened at the beginning of the engagement.
- The understanding of "right" product may evolve with time as business gains better understanding themselves, and the market continues to evolve.

Regular interaction with business stakeholders helps the team stay current with the market needs and helps build the product that is valuable (not just usable).

2.3   Proactive Prioritization

The user requirements must be processed strictly in order of priority, during development and also during the value discovery stage. This implies an important work discipline for the Product Owner/Manager as they need to constantly prioritize work and defer discussions with stakeholders on any requirements not expected to be picked up for development in next 1-2 months. In other words, the Simplicity Principle (#10 in Agile Manifesto) is equally relevant for value discovery stage.

Setting up a visual board can help Product Owners/Managers ensure a priority-based flow. Some concepts relevant here are Product Roadmap, Story Map, Discovery Kanban, MoSCoW model and Kano model.

3. Incremental Value Creation

An Agile team creates value incrementally, working on few high priority requirements at a time rather than committing to a big batch of requirements. An incremental approach also helps team minimize waste in case business needs change in future which they almost always do. The five sub-practices below are integral to incremental value creation.

3.1 Defer Commitment by Limiting Work in Progress

While a team adopting the Waterfall process starts the entire scope of work and does one activity at a time (in sequential order), an Agile team commits to a small amount of work and aims to finish all activities (Analysis, Planning, Design, Development, Testing and Delivery) within a short timeframe. The key idea is to commit to a small amount of work that is most valuable and well understood, then defer commitment on the rest of the scope that is relatively less valuable and can wait for now.

This set of activities (from analysis to delivery) are repeated for one set of features after another, over and over again (see picture).

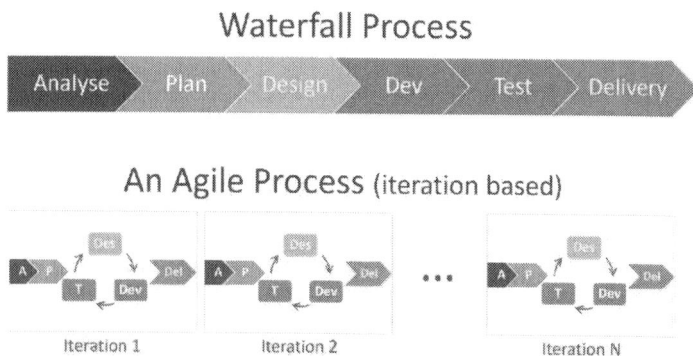

Waterfall Process

An Agile Process (iteration based)

| Iteration 1 | Iteration 2 | Iteration N |

This incremental approach allows the team to:

- Keep a narrow focus on work
- Shorten the learning cycle – Learning continuously from the completed work
- Adapt the product – by refining the scope of work to maximize value
- Reflect on the current process and evolve it continuously
- Minimize waste by not spending efforts on uncommitted scope as it might change in future

Now, the question naturally arises – how to decide the size of this timeframe and how much work to commit to?

A concept commonly used in Kanban community is "match demand with capability" – commit to a small scope of work (demand) for a short timeframe based the team's capability (not capacity). In Scrum, it amounts to deciding the Sprint length (2 weeks to a month) and pulling in work based on team's velocity (capability). In Kanban, the same may be accomplished by replenishing the input queue on a weekly basis based on average weekly throughput.

This idea of deferring commitment is closely related to three other key Agile concepts:

3.2 Adaptive Planning

This is an incremental approach to planning where team plans and commits to a small set of work items that will keep them busy for the next one or few weeks. This planning and execution cycle repeats one after another. The team first inspects the progress made so far, reviews the changed landscape of requirements and adapts as needed.

3.3   Emergent Design

A key technical practice in Extreme Programming (XP) methodology, the idea of Emergent Design is to take an incremental approach to design and architecture of the system – quite opposite to the traditional 'big design up front' approach where the team spends considerable effort to finalize (and often freeze) the design of the entire system before any development effort can be started.

3.4   Priority Based Flow

While it is important that requirements flow to the team in prioritized order, it is equally important that development team pays attention to work items while they are being worked on. This helps ensure:

- Items are picked based on business priority order rather than personal comfort
- Higher priority items pass through the workflow faster compared to other items
- Team pays regular attention to items that are blocked or held up so they are not delayed for too long
- Team pays attention to new information that may have an impact on business priority of items currently in progress

3.5   Implement Faster Feedback Cycles

One of the key motivations of an incremental process is to enable early feedback so any defects or shortcomings can be rectified in a timely manner. Some related terms often used are 'test fast', 'fail fast' and 'reject fast'. My personal preference is the term 'learn fast'.

Below are some of the common feedbacks sought in an agile development process:

i. Developer testing
ii. Code integration
iii. Code review
iv. QA Testing
v. Product Owner review
vi. Review by customer/business
vii. UAT testing
viii. End user feedback (after product deployment)

The idea of faster feedback is to bring all these feedbacks as close to development as possible. If a team that deploys to production once a quarter starts their UAT testing 10-15 days before the release date, it is probably too late because a feature that was developed in the first week is waiting for almost two months before it is picked up for UAT. Sometimes there could be constraints, but the team must consider improving their agility by starting UAT testing in the first month itself. This will enable the team to get the UAT feedback in a timely manner without causing any last moment chaos.

Continuous Integration (CI) is another important practice to enable timely feedback – this practice mandates developers merge their code into a common repository at regular intervals, followed by an automated build (and tests) to ensure new changes work well with the existing code. Developers are encouraged to integrate their code after completion of small bits of functionality, and not wait until the completion of an entire feature or story.

Continuous Integration helps ensure that the sanity of the codebase is maintained at all times to prevent the "integration hell" situation that was common in waterfall projects.

An important note – some teams follow the practice of nightly builds which could be good enough based on where they are coming from, but is not frequent enough. It is a sub-optimal approach as integration issues stay hidden during the daytime and often drain entire team's energy the next morning after a build failure.

4. Frequent Value Delivery

One of the primary motivations for most organizations that transition to Agile is to be able to release early and often. This ensures faster returns on investment. Below are some key practices that enable a team deliver early and often.

4.1 Regular completion of usable features

To enable frequent value delivery to customer, it is essential that team completes usable features on a regular basis. Two key points here:

1. The focus here is finishing usable features, not just individual work items. This requires team's effort is aligned to business needs and team members collaborate to ensure faster completion of related work items.
2. Team members must not complete work items in a rush, but finish them with high quality –ideally ready to go live. Mature teams use an explicit checklist to help team members self-manage their efforts and finish work items with a consistent quality.

4.2 Test automation

Frequent value delivery means frequent thorough testing of the product – not just new features, but also existing features to ensure they have not been impacted by the new work.

Automating the testing activities (unit tests, integration tests, etc.) not only saves time and money, it also minimizes the possibility of human errors.

4.3 Regular feedback from stakeholders

Rather than waiting until the end, an Agile team showcases the completed work to stakeholders on a regular basis, to ensure their efforts are aligned with business needs. The team could either establish a platform where stakeholders can directly view the completed features as they are marked done by the team, or they can have a defined cadence where team formally demos a batch of completed work to the stakeholders (Sprint Review in Scrum).

4.4 Automated deployment

Just like test automation, automating deployment process saves time and effort associated with deploying solution to a specific environment, while minimizing possibility of human errors. It also reduces dependency on specialists (ops team) who are often thinly spread across multiple projects/programs.

5. Continuous Improvement

An Agile team owns their development process and aims to continuously evolve it over time.

5.1 Daily Connect

Perhaps the most common feature of an Agile team, irrespective of the framework, this is the daily team coordination meeting that is usually time-boxed to 15-minutes and is held at the start of the day. Here, the team quickly inspects work completed in last 24 hours and the overall progress so far, and plans/re-plans work for the next 24 hours. It is often called a 'standup' meeting as team members are expected to stand through it to keep the meeting short and crisp.

Intention being the same, the exact format of this meeting may vary from one Agile framework to another. Two of the most common formats are member sharing updates in a round-robin order and team lead/coach walking the visual board.

5.2 Regular 'kaizen' events

Agile teams practice 'kaizen' culture – the culture of continuously improving the ways things are done. Some say 'kaizen' is a work ethic, a state of mind that needs to be practiced regularly. Conducting frequent kaizen events helps a team practice and embrace this culture.

In Scrum, Sprint Retrospective provide the platform where teams inspect and adapt their process. Kanban Method proposes multiple review meetings that allow improvement opportunities for the teams, most notably the Service Delivery Review at team level and Operations Review for a multi-team scenario where representatives from different teams meet to review and improve their inter-team coordination of information and dependencies.

Below is pictorial representation of the five Agile disciplines and the associated practices:

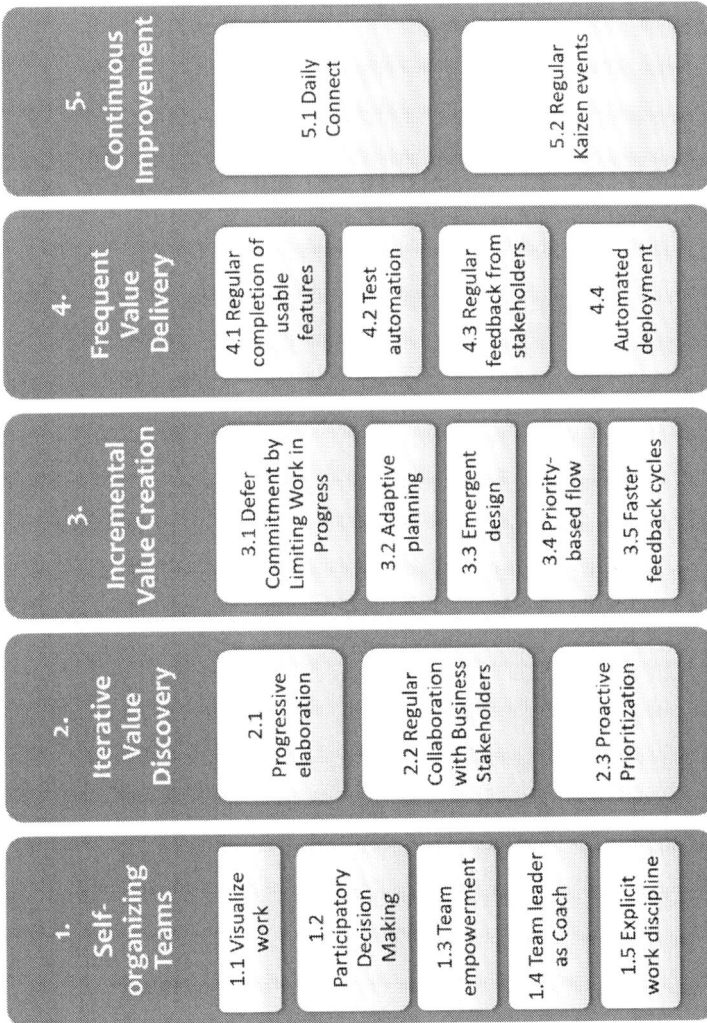

1. Self-organizing Teams	2. Iterative Value Discovery	3. Incremental Value Creation	4. Frequent Value Delivery	5. Continuous Improvement
1.1 Visualize work	2.1 Progressive elaboration	3.1 Defer Commitment by Limiting Work in Progress	4.1 Regular completion of usable features	5.1 Daily Connect
1.2 Participatory Decision Making	2.2 Regular Collaboration with Business Stakeholders	3.2 Adaptive planning	4.2 Test automation	5.2 Regular Kaizen events
1.3 Team empowerment	2.3 Proactive Prioritization	3.3 Emergent design	4.3 Regular feedback from stakeholders	
1.4 Team leader as Coach		3.4 Priority-based flow	4.4 Automated deployment	
1.5 Explicit work discipline		3.5 Faster feedback cycles		

5. Essence of Scrum Framework

Scrum is often described as a lightweight process framework that is simple to understand but difficult to master. It evolved in 1990s for managing software product development and now is considered the most popular and most widely adopted framework to implement Agile. In fact, it is so popular that many organizations start their agile journey with the assumption that 'Agile = Scrum'.

Given the popularity of Scrum, there are good chances you might already be familiar with it – either through books, some internal training or a public certification training. If you are not, it is highly recommended that you review the latest version of Scrum Guide. This chapter is intended to serve as a quick summary of Scrum (based on Scrum Guide 2017), with some useful tips, but not a comprehensive guide to help you transition to Scrum.

At a very high level, Scrum can be broken down into the following components:

- Values – Commitment, Courage, Openness, Focus and Respect
- Sprint – A fixed timebox 2 weeks to 1 month long where team focuses on achieving a well-defined business goal.
- 3 Roles – Scrum Master, Product Owner, Development Team

- 5 events – Sprint, Sprint Planning, Daily Scrum, Sprint Review and Sprint Retrospective
- 3 Artifacts – Product Backlog, Sprint Backlog and Product Increment

The Idea of Sprint

The idea of Sprint is the core of Scrum; it binds everything together. Let us try to understand the idea and the motivations behind it:

- **Fixed timebox:** Sprint duration is usually 2 weeks, 3 weeks, 4 weeks or a month and is expected to stay the same from one sprint to another. While 2 weeks is the most common Sprint duration, a team must choose what works best for them.
- **Fixed Goal for the Sprint:** The key idea of a timebox is to commit to a specific amount of work that is aligned to some business goal and finish it before the Sprint ends. While the scope of work may go through changes, the Sprint goal is expected to stay the same. Significant changes in Sprint goal during Sprint may call for a need to cancel the current Sprint and start a fresh one.
- **Prioritize finishing:** A clear goal for a short, fixed timebox helps align entire team's efforts and brings a sense of urgency enabling faster completion of work items.
- **Inspect and Adapt culture:** Sprint enforces a continuous improvement culture by providing multiple opportunities to inspect and adapt the product as well as the process.

Scrum Roles

Scrum provides a clear and precise description of three roles that are engineered to promote value-delivery focus and self-organizing culture.

Product Owner (PO)

PO is responsible for maximizing the value of the product resulting from work of the Development Team and focuses on building the right product, and the most valuable product.

Here are the key responsibilities of the Product Owner:

1. Manage stakeholder expectations
2. Develop Product Vision and Strategy
3. Create and Maintain Product Backlog
4. Maintain positive working relationship with Dev team
5. Help Dev team own and maximize business value delivery

Development Team

Dev Team consists of all members who directly contribute in converting backlog items to product increment – UI designers, architects, developers, testers, DBA's, etc.

Here are the key characteristics of a Dev Team:

1. **Small Team:** Team size is limited to 3 to 9 members.
2. **Flat Team Hierarchy:** Within the Dev Team, each person is a Team Member. Scrum does not encourage additional roles such as Developer, Tester, Architect, Senior Developer, etc.
3. **Cross-functional:** Team has all the skills (design, dev, test, etc.) to convert requirements (product backlog) into product increment.

4. **Self-Organizing:** Scrum empowers the Dev Team to do all decision making necessary for creating the next product increment.

5. **Collective Team Ownership:** While each member may have their individual work commitments, the team has collective ownership (and accountability) on the product increment, and thus are expected to help each other and hold each other accountable throughout the Sprint.

Scrum Master (SM)

Scrum Master is team's coach, not a manager. She is expected to work as an enabler for the team – an enabler for sustainable pace, good quality and overall team growth. A common phrase used to describe Scrum Master role is 'servant leader' – a leader whose focus is to serve the goal/purpose of the team, rather than expecting the team to serve her own purpose (quick promotion?).

Here are the key responsibilities of a Scrum Master (not in priority order):

1. Acquire expert knowledge on Agile
2. Foster an effective working relationship between PO and Dev team
3. Facilitate team meetings effectively
4. Help team track their work in a timely manner
5. Remove impediments and unnecessary distractions
6. Establish collaborative team environment
7. Promote High performance team culture

Business Value Delivery using Scrum

As we discussed in previous chapters, the key focus of Agile is to use an empirical process that helps a team maximize value delivery to the customer. The entire value delivery process can be broken down into three key overlapping phases – Value Discovery, Value Creation and Value Delivery.

Value Discovery Process in Scrum

Below are the key concepts in Scrum that help us with the value discovery process:

1. **Product Owner:** Coordinates with the business/customer, subject matter experts (SMEs) and end users to ensure the team develops deeper insights about the market needs and identify product requirements in a timely manner.

2. **Product Backlog (PBL):** The list of requirements arranged in the order of priority. The requirements at the top are in strict order of priority and are more granular – almost ready to be picked by the dev team. While the team may help create requirements and maintain the product backlog, it is owned by the Product Owner. In contrast to the waterfall process where requirements are frozen before development starts, the product backlog is a dynamic entity – the discovery, refinement and prioritization of requirements happens continuously in parallel with development.

3. **User Story format:** Though not an original idea of Scrum, most Scrum teams use user stories to describe user needs (requirements). The story format has two parts:
    o   **Story title:** As a <role> I want<functionality> so that <value proposition>

- o **Acceptance criteria:** List of functionality expectations that is used to validate and accept that story has been completed.

4. **Backlog Refinement:** Since the product backlog is a dynamic entity that continues to evolve as the project (or product development) progresses, we need a mechanism to ensure that team is aware of the changes and understands them well. Most Scrum teams conduct Backlog Refinement meeting once or twice per Sprint to ensure just that. PO shares details on the highest priority backlog items with the team that are expected to be pulled for development in the upcoming Sprint. The Dev Team tries to understand the requirements, refine the acceptance criteria as needed and estimates the size of backlog items (in Story points).

Value Creation Process in Scrum

In Scrum, value creation takes place inside short timeboxed iterations called "Sprint". A Sprint is a fixed timebox of 1 month or less, with focus on creating a potentially releasable product increment. Below is the sequence of key activities in a Sprint:

1. **Sprint Planning:** Usually a 2 to 4 hour meeting, here the team forecasts the functionality that can be done in the current Sprint and then plans for it using collaborative decision making (to be facilitated by Scrum Master):

   a. Product Owner comes with a prioritized backlog with the top few stories already understood and refined by the team (backlog refinement meeting). If not, team would spend time here to understand, refine and estimate the size of stories. The PO may also share the Sprint Goal at this point.

b. Team pulls the top priority story from PBL and validates its readiness (DoR - Definition of Ready)

c. If the story is ready to be started, the team plans for it:

- The story is broken into multiple small tasks.
- Team members pull tasks based on their availability, confidence and interest.
- Team members share their time estimate for their individual tasks. If the task estimate is more than a day, it may need to be broken into smaller tasks.
- Once all tasks have been identified, assigned and estimated, the story is marked as complete.

d. Stories are pulled from PBL and steps (b) and (c) are repeated for each until all team members have exhausted most of their capacity. Teams usually reserve 10%-30% of each member's capacity to take care of any future uncertainties.

e. Team's task board (electronic and/or physical board) is set up showing all stories and tasks committed for the Sprint.

2. **Sprint Execution:** Soon after the planning, the team members start picking up individual tasks (one by one), with a focus to finish stories in priority order.

3. **Daily Scrum:** This is a daily event time-boxed to 15-minutes, usually held at the start of the day. Here, the team quickly inspects work done since last Daily Scrum and the overall progress towards the Sprint goal, and plans work for the next 24 hours. If done effectively, the Daily Scrum optimizes the probability of team meeting the Sprint Goal.

4. **Sprint Review:** Held on the last day of the Sprint, here the Scrum team inspects the Product Increment with the stakeholders and adapts the Product Backlog if needed. This

is an informal meeting to seek timely feedback from stakeholders and foster trust and collaboration.

It is recommended that team members are encouraged to demonstrate the functionality to stakeholders rather than the Product Owner doing it. Besides empowering the team, it improves the sense of ownership on the product and overall team commitment.

5. **Sprint Retrospective:** This is an opportunity for the Scrum Team to continuously evolve their process by inspecting their experience in the previous Sprint, learning from it and planning small improvements in the next one. It could be a difficult meeting to facilitate if the team had a bad Sprint and will require Scrum Master to possess expert facilitation skills – so she can enable positive team dynamics and ensure each team member participates actively without fear or restraint.

Value Delivery Process in Scrum

After the dev team has created value for the customer, it must be delivered to the end user at an earliest possible opportunity. A delay between value creation and value delivery may be seen as a possible loss of business opportunity.

Three concepts that support a culture of frequent delivery in Scrum are:

- **Sprint Review:** As explained in the previous section, it provides an opportunity for 'value confirmation', an important prerequisite for value delivery. It ensures team efforts are in alignment with stakeholder expectations – that Dev team has built what really matters.

- **Potentially Releasable Product Increment:** At the end of each Sprint, the Dev Team is expected to have an enhanced version of the product (Product Increment) that is potentially releasable to production.

- **Definition of Done (DoD):** Think of this as a checklist of activities (exit criteria) that must be done by the Dev team for each backlog item to ensure it has been 'Done' as per team's own expectations. While acceptance criteria describe what functionality needs to be developed, DoD talks about the team's work discipline – it may cover concerns related to code reviews, code quality, unit tests, code coverage, etc.

How to choose Sprint length?

Most Scrum implementations start with management pushing down for Sprint length of 2 weeks. Their reasoning being – "When the rest of the world can follow 2-week Sprints, why can't you?"

In my experience, how to decide Sprint length is a poorly understood concept. There is no doubt that we must go for a shorter timebox (2-week) rather than longer (3- or 4-week) wherever possible, but we need to consider existing team challenges. Two commonly considered guideline are the pace of new requirements inflow and the desired frequency of product demo to the customer.

Another important consideration that is often overlooked is the time required to complete an average work item. Here, we are talking about the cycle time or the elapsed time for an item from start to finish, not effort spent in hours/days. The sprint length should be roughly double the average cycle time of medium sized items or more.

Let us take an example – consider a new Scrum team that has estimated their stories in the range of 1 point to 8 points. If their high-level estimate for completing a 5 point story (including testing) is 6 days or less, I would go for a 2-week Sprint; if it is 7-12 days, probably a 3-week Sprint; anything higher, a 4-week Sprint would make better sense.

The reasoning behind this approach is that if most work items take longer than 60% of the Sprint length, work items would tend to pile up for testing towards the end of the Sprint – leading to unnecessary panic in last 2-3 days – somewhat similar to the chaos in the last 1-2 months of a waterfall project. This is often termed as 'waterfall in a Sprint'.

If the team is new and there is high uncertainty about requirements, technical challenges and/or team dynamics, one option could be to try Kanban for a month with weekly replenishment, learn from that experience and decide the Sprint length accordingly. Please see next chapter to understand how Kanban could be used for development projects.

Summary of Scrum

Key Strengths of Scrum

- ✓ **Simple to understand:** While there are detailed 2-day trainings, the key elements of Scrum may well be explained in less than an hour.
- ✓ **Well-structured Sprint cadence:** Good guidance on how to get started, what meetings to conduct, when and for how long.
- ✓ **Clarity on Roles:** Very clear and precise description of three roles.

✓ **Emphasis on small Cross-Functional teams:** Insisting on cross-functional teams is a path-breaking idea that reduces hand-offs and delays in feedback – an essential enabler for incremental development.

✓ **Emphasis on Collaboration:** Scrum ceremonies are well structured to promote regular team collaboration.

✓ **Promotes *kaizen* culture:** The idea of short sprints combined with the structure of ceremonies provide regular 'inspect and adapt' opportunities, promoting the culture of continuous improvement.

Common implementation challenges

While Scrum is easy to understand, it takes time to adapt to the Sprint cadence:

1. **Difficult transition to Scrum Master role** – While it may look easy on paper, the transition to Scrum Master role is a big mindset shift, and often requires quite a bit of unlearning old behaviour. The most common dysfunction among new Scrum Masters is to behave like a manager or architect rather than a team coach – thereby playing active role in decision making, pushing team members, or interact with team only during Daily Scrum.

2. **Big learning curve for proactive collaboration** – Frequent and timely collaboration requires self-discipline among team members and it usually takes time before team members proactively start seeking requirement clarifications, report blockers, or seek help from others.

3. **Team not able to finish all committed stories** – It is natural that a new Scrum team takes time to adjust to the idea of Sprint and find a good rhythm. But, if the management or the

customer starts reacting negatively to the team missing their Sprint forecast, it could create an unhealthy and unsafe team environment.

4. **Handling scope changes during Sprint** – Most Scrum teams struggle with handling scope changes that come during the Sprint. Many teams take an extreme approach – allow no changes once Sprint starts or let all changes come in. A more effective approach is that team discusses each incoming change to understand its value and urgency, evaluates the impact on current scope of work, negotiates the change with Product Owner and updates the Sprint plan if needed. Scrum Master needs to facilitate this negotiation between the Product Owner and the team.

Dysfunctional Scrum Implementations

Scrum is hard to implement as it brings a big change – changes in team structure and roles, alignment to Sprint cadence, collaborative work discipline, etc. Many organizations try to work around some of the necessary elements of Scrum and end up having a dysfunctional Scrum implementation:

1. **Waterfall in a Sprint**: This is probably the most common dysfunction among new Agile teams that are coming from a waterfall background. Each developer picks a story for the Sprint and gets is ready for testing around day 6-8. Testers try to keep themselves busy in the first week by finishing pending items from previous Sprint or preparing test cases for current stories. But good chances they are lightly loaded in the first two-third of the Sprint and overloaded in the last 2-3 days. Most committed items tend to finish in the last few

days only and those days are usually stressful for the entire team.

A simple way to spot this dysfunction is to look at your Sprint burnup chart (not burndown). It may look like the following:

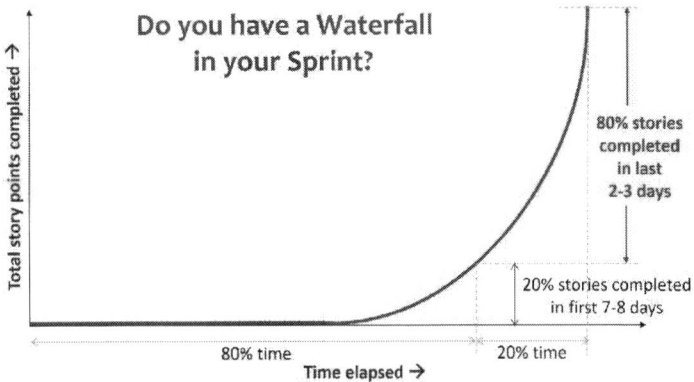

For solution ideas, see point# 3 in next section "Succeeding with Scrum". If defining smaller stories or executing them faster does not seem to work, team may consider increasing sprint length or switching to Kanban Method. After a few months, once the team has gained a better rhythm and is able to bring down cycle time for stories, team may reconsider using Scrum with shorter Sprint length.

2. **Waterfall across Sprints**: Developers and testers execute their separate Sprints, with Dev Sprint feeding work to Test Sprint and Test Sprint feeding bugs to the Dev Sprint.

   Solution – revisit, relearn and retry the idea of cross-functional teams. There is simply no workaround if you wish to practice Scrum.

3. **Project Manager Reincarnation:** Product Owner and Scrum Master roles played by the same person, usually the erstwhile

Project Manager. This puts too much authority with one person – a huge risk to team's self-organizing culture.

4. **Multiple Sprint 0's:** Team executes multiple Sprint 0 (zero) because they believe a lot of work needs to be done before the first Sprint can start that will produce a demo-ready Product Increment. Mostly this is the old waterfall thinking that perfect architectural platform must be ready before feature development can start. In other words, a resistance to the idea of 'emergent design'. As a coach, I would focus on right conversations and some training on concepts such as emergent design, 'walking skeleton', MMF (minimum marketable features), MVP (minimum viable product), etc.

Succeeding with Scrum

So, what makes teams succeed with Scrum? Below is my list of key pointers that could help:

1. **Pick the RIGHT Scrum Master candidate:** In my experience, if you can find a good Scrum Master, your chances of success would be much more than 50%. While many managers consider their transition to Scrum Master role a demotion, I consider it to be a more challenging role because influencing people is difficult than directing people. Influencing is even more difficult if one has been used to directing for several years. Here are some quick things to keep in mind while choosing a Scrum Master:
   - **Right personality**: Positivity (in behaviour and language), passion for excellence and perseverance to pursue results.
   - **Some seniority**, ideally peer level to Product Owner: Scrum Master should have some seniority, otherwise

team members, PO and/or management may not take her seriously. Rotating the Scrum Master roles among team members could be a risky proposition as it might undermine the importance of SM role.

- **Evaluate need for mentoring:** If Scrum Master is new to the role, mentoring by an experienced Agile Coach should be treated as a must have. The mentoring must focus on Scrum concepts and the idea of facilitative leadership.

2. **Shorter stories:** It is a good idea to define a max size (say, 5 or 8 points) for stories that can be pulled into a Sprint. Anything more than that must be split into smaller stories.

3. **Active collaboration among team members:** Scrum Master needs to act as an enabler for this:

- **Board must be live all the time** – a common rule is to update the board within '10 min' of completing the story/task.

- **Team members must collaborate throughout the day**, not only during team meetings. A common dysfunction among new Agile teams is that team members wait until next day's Daily Scrum to share impediments or seek help from others.

- **Encourage multiple developers to collaborate on a single story** – New Scrum teams coming from waterfall background usually continue their 'one developer per story' rule. Encouraging multiple developers collaborate on a single story helps improve cycle time, besides improving quality and code consistency.

- **Overlap development and testing efforts** – Another default (but flawed) practice that often comes from waterfall is 'testing starts after development is complete'. This practice slows down the feedback loop and limits interaction among developers and testers, thereby increasing item turnaround time and reducing team velocity. Testers must be encouraged to overlap their efforts with developers as much as possible – for example, by sharing their test cases with developers early and testing partially done stories (few acceptance criteria that have been developed).

4. **Implement metrics:** Most new teams take the metrics somewhat casually. Metrics are the key to Empiricism. They must be tracked and made visible, ideally next to the physical board. Here is a quick list of metrics:

- **Sprint burndown (hours planned)** – total pending work for the current Sprint. Updated at the end of Daily Scrum.

- **Sprint burnup (story points)** – total work completed till date. Updated at the end of Daily Scrum.

- **Velocity chart** – A bar chart showing historical team velocity and is updated at the end of each Sprint.

- **Release burnup (story points)** – This metric is used when team deploys to production after every few several Sprints. This is updated at the end of each Sprint and would usually have a target line that could also change with time.

Mapping Scrum Concepts with key Agile Practices

Below is an attempt to map key Scrum concepts/practices with the Agile practices discussed in chapter 4:

Agile Practice	Scrum Concept/Practice
1. Self-Organizing Teams	
1.1 Visualize work	* Task Board
1.2 Participatory Decision Making	* Scrum Master as facilitator * Whole team presence in meetings
1.3 Team empowerment	* Dev Team owns delivery * Flat team hierarchy * Team pulls work
1.4 Team leader as Coach	* Scrum Master as servant leader
1.5 Explicit work discipline	* Definition of Ready * Definition of Done
2. Iterative Value Discovery	
2.1 Progressive elaboration	* Emergent Product Backlog * Backlog refinement
2.2 Regular Collaboration with Business Stakeholders	* Sprint Review * Dedicated role (PO) for customer interaction
2.3 Proactive Prioritization	* Prioritized Product Backlog

3. Incremental Value Creation	
3.1 Defer Commitment by Limiting Work in Progress	* Sprint timebox * Limited scope for Sprint
3.2 Adaptive planning	* Sprint Planning
3.3 Emergent design	
3.4 Priority-based flow	* Sprint
3.5 Faster feedback cycles	* Cross functional team * Definition of Done * Burndown/Burnup chart * PO review stories as they are completed
4. Frequent Value Delivery	
4.1 Regular completion of usable features	* Sprint (Goal based batch flow) * Potentially releasable Product Increment * Definition of Done
4.2 Test automation	
4.3 Regular feedback from stakeholders	* Sprint Review
4.4 Automated deployment	
5. Continuous Improvement	
5.1 Daily Connect	* Daily Scrum
5.2 Regular Kaizen events	* Sprint Review * Sprint Retrospective

6. Essence of Kanban Method

Before we begin, a quick note – Kanban Method is not the same as kanban system used by Toyota Production System (TPS) in 1960s and 1970s. While it takes inspiration from TPS kanban, among many other work management concepts, Kanban Method is an evolved version, adapted specifically for knowledge work industry. In this chapter, when we mention Kanban (with capital K), we are talking about Kanban Method.

The other important point to understand is that Kanban Method is much more than just visualization (kanban board). It has values, principles, practices (visualization being one of them), roles, metrics, standard meetings (cadence) and more. In this chapter, we will cover the key essence of Kanban Method. For a deep dive, readers must consider books by David Anderson and Mike Burrows.

Why Kanban?

While most of the world transitions to Agile with the assumption Agile=Scrum, why talk about Kanban at all?

While Scrum is a useful framework with wide applicability, in some situations it may not be the best fit and in some cases it could prove to be a costly mistake.

According to popular belief, Kanban is good **only** for support/operations projects. The reality is that Kanban is good **even** for support/operations projects. Kanban has much wider applicability than commonly believed and can often be used for any project.

Below are some typical use cases where Kanban proves to be an effective option for development projects:

1. **A development project, transitioning from Waterfall to Agile**

When team feels Scrum is a big change and will likely cause confusion or chaos.

2. **In the beginning of a new development project**

When the new team is yet to find a rhythm for their value discovery and value creation process.

3. **For a mature product, with a mix of planned and unplanned work**

Or, any development project with significant amount of unplanned work (defects/CRs)

4. **For a mature Agile team, ready for Continuous Delivery**

When there is a need for item-based flow rather than batch flow, hence the completed items can be deployed to production independently.

Key Essence of Kanban Flow

What makes Kanban Method a viable option for most knowledge work project is its adaptive and continuous flow of work:

- **Continuous flow of work** – There are no start-stop iterations in Kanban. It practices Continuous flow of work.

- **Item-based flow** – Work items flow independently rather than as a batch, except when they have strong inter-dependencies.
- **Pull over Push** – Team pulls work when they have capacity available, rather than work being pushed to them based on customer demand. This is often a tough sell to managers who find it difficult to trust their team and fear the pull mechanism will lead to poor resource utilization.
- **Adaptive Demand Inflow cadence** – While most product development teams pull work once every week, it is perfectly okay to pull in urgent requests as they arrive during the week. While Kanban offers flexibility to pull in work as needed, it advocates it is done in a disciplined manner, so the dynamic inflow does not disrupt team's rhythm or pace.
- **Decoupled Delivery cadence** – the delivery cadence is decoupled from demand inflow cadence. A new dev team could be pulling requests into the flow every Monday morning, but delivering to production once per month. On the other hand, a mature dev team practicing continuous delivery could be pulling in requests dynamically and delivering individual items as and when they are done.
- **Powerful metrics** – Continuous flow of work warrants continuous monitoring of work progress to ensure team can sustain its pace and rhythm. Kanban Method provides powerful flow-based metrics that help teams measure and improve predictability of pace (throughput) and turnaround time (cycle/lead time).

Values and Principles behind Kanban Method

Kanban Values

Kanban embraces 9 core values – Transparency, Balance, Collaboration, Customer Focus, Flow, Leadership, Understanding, Agreement and Respect.

There are two set of principles identified in Kanban Method – Change Management Principles and Service Delivery Principles.

Change Management Principles

1. Start with what you do now:
   a. Understand current processes, as actually practiced
   b. Respect existing roles, responsibilities, and job titles
2. Gain agreement to pursue improvement through evolutionary change.
3. Encourage acts of leadership at all levels.

Service Delivery Principles

1. Understand and focus on the customer's needs and expectations.
2. Manage the work; let people self-organize around it.
3. Regularly review the network and its policies to improve outcomes.

Core Practices in Kanban Method

Below is a quick summary of the six core practices identified in Kanban Method:

1. Visualize work

Knowledge work is usually hidden (in hard disks or human memory), and requires that you ask people to understand the current status. The practice of visualization uses a kanban board to improve transparency about how much work is in progress, at what state, who is working on what, what is blocked, and so on. Mature teams also visualize their work-related policies on the board.

The first step towards designing a kanban board is to understand how work flows from start (commitment point) to finish, with each column representing a sequential activity or a waiting stage. Multiple activities that happen in parallel may be combined in a single column.

Here is a simple kanban board I have seen many development teams use:

Backlog	Input Queue	Development		Testing	Done
		Doing	Done		

Another example of kanban board for a development project, with a slightly different flow of work:

Backlog	Input Queue	Back-end		Front-end		QA	UAT	Ready to Deploy
		Doing	Done	Doing	Done			

Here is a sample kanban board for an IT support project:

Request Backlog	Prioritized	Analysis	In Progress		Review	Ready to Deploy	Deployed
			Doing	Done			

Below is a simple kanban board that can be used for non-IT project (say HR team) or for one individual (personal Kanban):

Backlog	Input Queue	In Progress	Done

2. Limit WIP (work in progress)

As discussed previously, limiting work in progress ensures team maintains a narrow focus that will help them prioritize finishing of work items – leading to a predictable pace and turnaround time. A phrase used often in Kanban is "stop starting, start finishing". I sometimes use a different phrase to highlight this work discipline – "you touch it, you finish it".

A common question is 'how to decide WIP limits'?

While there are ways to arrive at the starting WIP limit, finding a suitable WIP limit is an empirical process that requires continuous inspection and adaptation. The common rule is – if you find work often waiting for people, reduce WIP limit; if people often wait for work, increase WIP limit.

3. Manage flow

Maintaining a healthy flow of work requires active monitoring so we can prevent (or fix) two common challenges associated with continuous flow:

- Bottleneck – Work waiting for people
- Starvation – People waiting for work

While visualization of work, metrics and meetings provide key structure in managing the flow, please note that it is an ongoing activity that must be owned by the team and facilitated by the team coach.

4. Make policies explicit

Explicit policies define entry and exit criteria for different activities in an unequivocal manner, helping the team develop a shared understanding of how to do a great job. Besides reducing confusion about the process specifics, they help ensure consistent quality across team members.

In Scrum, definition of Ready (DoR) and definition of done (DoD) define entry and exit criteria for the entire workflow, whereas explicit policies in Kanban are at a more granular level – for each activity or column.

5. Implement feedback loops

Feedback loops provide team an opportunity to 'inspect and adapt'. Contrary to popular belief, Kanban has multiple feedback loops – Daily Kanban, Service Delivery Review, Operations Review and Risk Review. Please see the section 'Team Meetings in Kanban Method' for further details.

6. Improve collaboratively, evolve experimentally

As mentioned before, two common challenges with flow of work are bottlenecks and starvation. Kanban encourages teams to treat these challenges as an opportunity for improvement, collaborate in decision making and take an evidence-based approach for continuous improvement. That sounds very much aligned with the thought process behind Agile.

Some popular management models often referenced in Kanban are Theory of Constraints (ToC), System of Profound Knowledge (Edward Deming), Queuing Theory, Cost of Delay and Economic Costs model.

Additional Kanban Concepts

Work Item Types

Work item types are segregation of work into different categories based on how they are processed. A real-life example – work item types for a courier service could be envelope, box, tube, perishables, freight, etc.

For a development team, the common work item types are production defects, change requests and new features. For an IT support team, work item types could be incident, service request, production defect, routine maintenance, etc.

Class of Service (CoS)

Defining classes of service is segregation of work based on urgency or cost of delay. Classes of service for a courier service could be – standard, priority, express, overnight, same-day, etc.

Kanban Method lists four classes of service:

1. **Standard:** By default, unless there is a specific need, each work item assumes standard urgency.
2. **Fixed Date:** For items that need to be done by a certain date, that may be difficult to achieve with Standard CoS, team may consider upgrading them to 'Fixed Date' CoS. A fixed date item has a due date – that is linked to an anticipated reward or penalty.
3. **Expedite:** This is the highest class of service – indicating that the cost of delay is extremely high. The highest possible urgency. Think of a production server going down or a production defect that could cause security loophole in a banking application.
4. **Intangible:** These are work items with low perceived value (for the customer), and lower cost of delay. Hence the lowest class of service. Think of technical work items – refactoring code, improving automation test coverage, taking care of technical debt, version upgrade, etc. that the development

team will value greatly but may not be the top priority for the business.

These four usually are relevant and sufficient in most cases, but it is okay if Kanban practitioners feel the need to create a new class of service.

Swim Lanes

Swim lanes are horizontal partitions of the physical board that help in improving focus of the team, especially useful when the number of items in progress exceed beyond 10 or so, possibly cluttering the visual board. The most common approach is to use swim lanes for different types of work, with an additional lane (usually the top one) for Expedite items.

Here is an example board for a product development team that works on different types of work:

	Input Queue	Development		Testing	Done
		Doing	Done		
Expedite ⇨					
Production Defects ⇨					
Change Requests ⇨					
New Features ⇨					

Sometimes swim lanes are also used to bring multiple small teams working for the same program onto the same board, with each team focusing on a separate swim lane. Besides the convenience of tracking the entire program on a single board, it also helps shared resources (if any) get a better clarity on their individual work in progress.

Estimation in Kanban

Good chances you may have heard that Kanban Method recommends 'no estimates' – that you should not estimate work. This is a myth, probably because many Kanban practitioners have chosen that path, seemed to have liked it and have spread that idea.

The reality is that Kanban Method lets you choose an estimation approach that works for you. The 'no estimate' approach works well when there is very little variance in item sizes. The logic behind 'no estimates' approach is to take the time dimension out, so people are not biased by it (Parkinson's Law).

While 'no estimates' may work perfectly well for support projects, in my experience, development teams usually do not like the idea of 'no estimates'. They feel it is an inaccurate representation of how much work was completed.

Here is an estimation approach that has worked for me across various development projects using Kanban Method:

1. **Use relative estimation:** Estimate in timeless units – story point estimation or T-shirt sizing.
2. **Estimate size (output), not effort (input):** To get a better clarity on this, please refer appendix topic 'Estimation Approach in Agile'.
3. **Keep the estimation range small:** For T-shirt size, try to limit estimates within the S-M-L range, and for story point

estimation, limit estimates to 5 points. Any item more than 'L' or 5 points must be seen as a candidate for splitting down into smaller items.

Kanban Metrics

Metrics have two parts – what to measure (data) and how to visualize it (charts).

Below are some of the key measurements that can help Kanban teams track the effectiveness of their workflow:

1. **Throughput:** Amount of work completed by the team in a given time period (day, week or month). It may be calculated as number of items completed or number of story points completed (weighted throughput) if a team is practising story point estimation.

2. **Cycle Time (aka System Lead Time):** Elapsed time from the moment team commits an item to when it is done by the team.

3. **Lead Time (aka Customer Lead Time):** Elapsed time from the moment an item is committed to the customer to when it is delivered to the customer.

4. **Work in Progress (WIP):** Total number of work items in a given state, column or the entire workflow. Please note it is not the same as WIP limit.

5. **Flow Efficiency:** A measure of what percentage of time a work item was being actively worked on while it was in the workflow. It can be roughly calculated as total effort spent on an item divided by cycle time or lead time (depending on the scope of measurement).

6. **Escaped Defects:** Number of defects that have escaped a specific stage. Common examples are QA defects (escaped development), UAT defects (escaped QA) and production defects (escaped the entire process). This could be measured per release, per time period or per unit.

Below is the list of common visualizations of flow data (charts) commonly known as Kanban metrics:

Throughput Chart

This is a bar chart that shows history of throughput over several weeks or months.

Below is an example throughput chart for a development team. What do you think – are they progressing towards sustainable throughput?

Weekly Throughput Chart

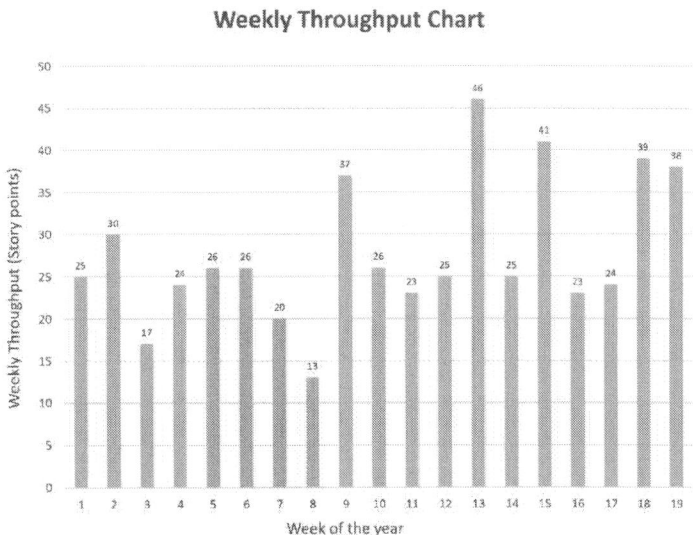

As a general guidance, less variance in throughput numbers

indicates a sign of maturity in team dynamics but we must not forget that variance will always be there for knowledge work.

Cumulative Flow Diagram (CFD)

This is perhaps the most widely known Kanban metric. Here we plot multiple lines, each representing total number of items that have crossed a specific stage (vertical line) in the workflow.

Quick guidance on how to interpret a CFD – the lines should maintain a healthy distance between them – two lines getting too close could be a sign of starvation (people waiting for work) while lines far apart means too much work in progress in a particular stage, a possibility of bottleneck.

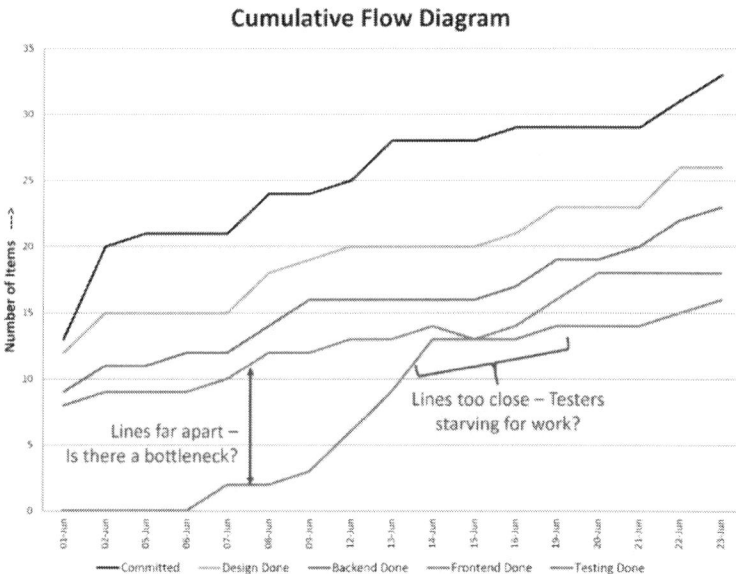

Cumulative Flow Diagram

Run Chart (Scatter Plot)

This is also known as Control Chart or Lead Time Scatter Plot. Here we plot the cycle time (or lead time) with respect to the date it was done. Each completed work item is represented as a dot on the chart.

Here we primarily look for spread of the plot – less spread (dots closer together) means more predictable flow. And, the closer the spread gets to X-axis, the better. In the sample chart below, the team seems to have improved a little over time as they are able to minimize the number of items with cycle time more than 10 days.

Run Chart

Cycle/Lead Time Distribution

An important metric but poorly supported by popular tools, this is a frequency distribution of cycle time (or lead time). It plots cycle time on X-axis and number of items with a specific cycle time on Y-axis.

In the two sample distributions below – which one do you think looks better?

Cycle Time Distribution

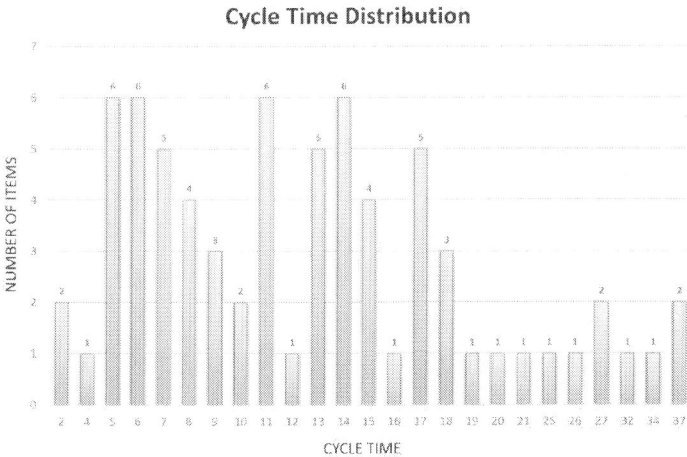

Cycle Time Distribution

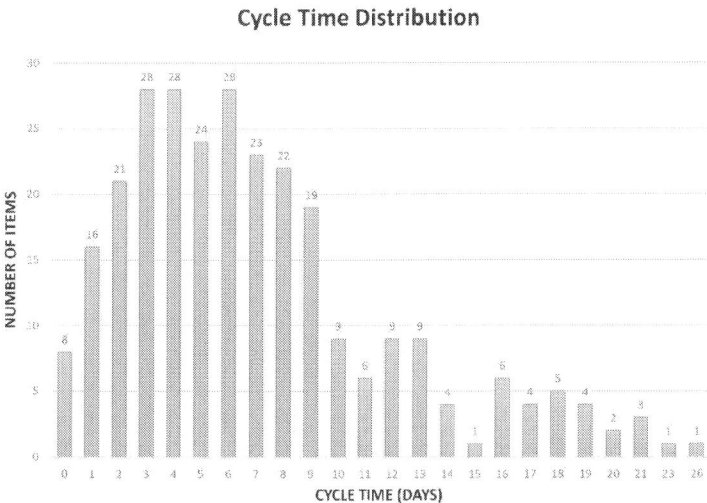

Quick guidance on Cycle Time distribution – a more concentrated distribution suggests less variance and more predictability. Three improvements opportunities a team must focus on to improve cycle time distribution are:

i. **Move Left:** Move the distribution to the left – finish items early.

ii. **Favour 'Tall and Narrow':** Squeeze the distribution to minimize the spread – 'tall and narrow' distribution is better than 'flat and wide'.

iii. **Trim or slim the tail:** Tail of the distribution denotes exceptions – items that were delayed due to lack of clarity, blockers, dependencies or poor craftmanship. And hence, are opportunities for improvement.

Flow Efficiency Distribution

Flow efficiency is perhaps the least commonly used and least understood Kanban metric due to the challenges in measuring it. One important thing to understand about flow efficiency is that – unlike other efficiency numbers – 100% is not an ideal goal here because 100% flow efficiency would mean absolutely no waiting time which could only happen in case of starvation. While one may desire 100% flow efficiency for super urgent (Expedite) items, more than 40% is a good number for standard items.

I have mostly seen Kanban practitioners talk about average flow efficiency and not talk about a specific visualization (chart). So, here I propose Flow Efficiency distribution as another useful Kanban metric – a frequency distribution just like Cycle Time distribution.

Below is an example of Flow Efficiency distribution:

Flow Efficiency Distribution

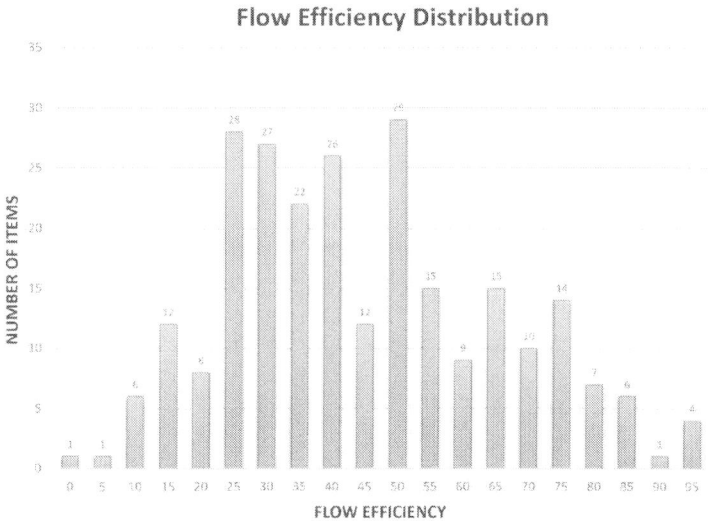

An important note: In contrast to the Cycle time distribution, to pursue improvements, here we would want to shift the distribution to the right (higher flow efficiency) and would try to trim/slim the tail on the left side of the curve.

Roles in Kanban Method

Kanban Method recommends two key roles:

Service Request Manager (SRM)

Very similar to Product Owner in Scrum, primary focus of SRM is value discovery – to analyse requests coming from customer/business, prioritize them and feed them to the delivery team strictly in order of priority. SRM may have their own Kanban board (discovery kanban) that shows the flow of requests from 'idea' stage to 'ready for engineering'.

Service Delivery Manager (SDM)

The focus of SDM is to ensure smooth and predictable flow of work by assisting the delivery team. While they are expected to facilitate team meetings like Scrum Master, an SDM is expected to have a stronger ownership on service delivery than a Scrum Master.

The definition of Kanban roles is a late addition, probably the reason for their low awareness and acceptance. In my experience, these roles are hard to find, even among mature Kanban teams. Add to that the 'manager' suffix that is often not liked by most agile coaches (the influencers).

Given the wider awareness and acceptance of Scrum roles, I have often seen Kanban teams continue with Scrum roles. Yes, a Scrum Master for a Kanban team.

Team Meetings in Kanban Method

As mentioned earlier, Kanban (Method) has team meetings that help teams plan, coordinate and improve how they work. Below is a quick summary of key Kanban meetings:

1. Daily Kanban

This is the daily team coordination meeting where the team reviews the overall progress and tries to unblock issues. Contrary to round-robin format of Daily Scrum, this is conducted in 'walk the board' format where team lead walks the board from right to left, focusing on key items that need team's attention, followed by team members sharing their concerns and challenges, if any.

2. Replenishment Meeting

Here the team reviews the list of requests with SRM and commits to work items (pulls onto the Kanban board). This meeting can be roughly compared to Sprint Planning meeting with some key differences:

- **Commitment to start, not to finish:** Recall that we have continuous flow of work in Kanban, which means that while we are replenishing the input queue, the rest of the flow is not empty – there are already some items that are in progress. Hence, the focus here is to pull in items that the team is expected to start this week once they are done with the current items.

- **Defer Commitment:** How much a team must commit to depends on their pace of work completion (throughput). This is called matching demand with capability. A common practice to pull little more than how much the team expects to finish until the next replenishment meeting. A little more than throughput to take care of natural variability in knowledge work, so the team does not have to call emergency Replenishment meeting in case some items get stuck or the team performs better than expectations.

- **Backlog refinement:** While Kanban Method does not talk explicitly about backlog refinement, most product development Agile teams find the idea very useful. With the development teams I have worked with, it is a common practice to include backlog refinement as a part of Replenishment meeting.

- **Meeting frequency:** The frequency of Replenishment meeting depends on the pace at which new requests arrive and the expected response time. For a support/operations project, with too many unplanned requests, team might practice dynamic replenishment where SRM keeps prioritized items ready in a column the team members can pull from when they have capacity. Most development teams that I have seen using Kanban conduct their replenishment once a week, except one that did once in a fortnight. So, the final word on replenishment cadence is – do what makes sense and works best for your team.

3. Service Delivery Review

Very similar to Sprint Retrospective, this is a meeting facilitated by SDM where team reviews and refines their process with a focus on improving both customer satisfaction and team dynamics. This is recommended to be done once every 2 weeks, but many Kanban teams in my experience do it once a month.

4. Operations Review

Operations review is an optional meeting relevant where multiple teams need to work in a collaborative manner – same product, program or business unit. Think of this as a multi-team retrospective where representatives from each team (SRM, SDM) come together to discuss their coordination challenges and pain points, and explore options to improve overall service delivery.

The recommendation is to do it monthly, to be facilitated by a senior manager responsible for the product, program or business unit.

There are three other meetings defined in Kanban Method but are less commonly used – Delivery Planning, Risk Review and Strategy Review.

Meeting Cadence Examples

Unlike Scrum, that gives a structured sequence of meetings, the team needs to design their cadence in Kanban. Depending on the maturity of the team, they may see it as a limitation or flexibility. Let us take a few examples and see how different events would be structured in Kanban.

1. **Development Team with Monthly Release Cycle**

Assuming a 4-week release cycle, here is the rough cadence of meetings:

- **Release Planning:** This is not a standard Kanban meeting, but I have seen most teams conduct this meeting to forecast the scope of work that can possibly be delivered in the upcoming release. While customer/management with waterfall mindset would push towards a strict commitment for an accurate scope, as an Agile practitioner you should go for rough forecasting. A better name for this meeting would probably be '*Release Forecast*'.
- **Replenishment meeting:** Once a week – day 1, 8, 15 and 21 (calendar days). Backlog refinement is done as a part of this meeting.
- **Daily Kanban:** Every day, of course.
- **Service Delivery Review:** Once around day 14 and the other next day after release is complete (and before next release starts).

- **Product Demo:** Not a standard Kanban meeting, but that does not mean we can't do it. I would recommend at least two demos – one towards the end of second week, and the second in fourth week, about 3-5 days before release so team has enough time to incorporate customer feedback.

2. Development Team with 3-Month Release Cycle

A 3 months release cycle would have 12 or 13 weeks and here is how the cadence of meetings would look like:

- **Release Planning/Forecast:** Once in the beginning, to forecast the scope of work that can possibly be delivered in the upcoming release. Since the amount uncertainty is higher for a 3 month release, an alternate approach could be to have a Release Forecast meeting at the beginning of each month where we inspect and adapt the release scope based on team's progress and changing priorities.
- **Replenishment meeting:** Once a week – any day of the week should be fine. Backlog refinement is done as a part of this meeting.
- **Daily Kanban:** Every day.
- **Service Delivery Review:** Once every 2-4 weeks. Most teams I have worked with opted for once every 4 weeks.
- **Product Demo:** Once every 2 weeks. Some teams may like to skip the first one if the number of completed items are low.

3. Development Team practicing Continuous Delivery

Here the assumption is items are deployed to production as they get ready, probably multiple times in a week.

- **Replenishment meeting:** For planned work, once a week – any day of the week is fine. Some unplanned work (production defects or change requests) is pulled in as needed, based on priority.

- **Daily Kanban:** Every day
- **Service Delivery Review:** Once in 2-4 weeks
- **Product Demo:** Formal demo is not required as individual items are made available to customer/business for review as they get ready.

4. IT Support Team
- **Replenishment meeting:** Dynamic replenishment as the inflow of requests is uncertain.
- **Daily Kanban:** Every day
- **Service Delivery Review:** Once in 2-4 weeks

Summary of Kanban Method

Key Strengths of Kanban Method

✓ **Evolutionary change approach:** Kanban is an evidence based evolutionary change approach that focuses on starting simple, addressing most pressing needs, then creating successful evidence, followed by an improvement cycle. Repeated over and over again.

✓ **Easy to get started:** Kanban does not mandate a rigid starting point. Most teams start with a physical Kanban board and daily standup, and slowly adopt other Kanban practices. While it may help, it is not mandatory to redefine roles or change team structure when you get started with Kanban.

✓ **More responsive to changes in the inflow:** Since there is no timebox, and no pressure to finish X amount of work items before a due date, Kanban teams are more open to accepting new unplanned work. But it is important to exercise some agreed discipline while accepting unplanned work, otherwise it may lead to high uncertainty in both throughput and turnaround time.

✓ **Powerful metrics:** Kanban has a comprehensive set of metrics – Cumulative Flow Diagram (CFD), Run Chart, Lead Time Distribution, Throughput Chart and Flow Efficiency. Together, they help enable Kanban's core idea of continuous improvement.

✓ **Wider applicability:** Contrary to the popular belief, Kanban can be adopted for almost any kind of project due to its flexibility and wide set of practices.

Common Implementation Challenges

- **Difficult to find Kanban expertise:** While Kanban Method has good set of practices and metrics, in my experience, it is extremely difficult to find Agile Coaches with deeper understanding of Kanban. It is even a bigger challenge when you expect them to have a good grip on Kanban metrics.

- **Complacency with initial improvement:** While it is easy to get started with Kanban and find initial improvement, it is common to see teams that stop right after visualization. Many don't even implement WIP limits. A primary reason for this is team's limited Kanban expertise (previous point), especially about Kanban metrics.

- **Poor support by popular tools:** While most popular Agile tools provide an option for Kanban, their support is somewhat limited. Some of the common options they do not support are splitting a column with a common WIP limit, WIP limits for Swim lanes, blocker stickies, and support for Lead

Time Distribution and Flow Efficiency. Two most mature Kanban tools are SwiftKanban and Kanbanize.

- **Lack of slack time:** The timebox element of Scrum provides a break, some slack time. The continuous flow of work in Kanban could get monotonous or tiring, depending on the pace of work. A good Team Coach needs to design some slack time into the process – perhaps a half day with events like such as service delivery review, product demo, technical knowledge sharing, team lunch, etc.

Succeeding with Kanban Method

So, what makes teams succeed with Kanban?

Below is a quick checklist (not a comprehensive one):

1. **Find an effective Team Coach:** Irrespective of the title (SDM, Kanban Master, Scrum Master, Manager), we need a team leader who had deeper knowledge of Kanban Method and carries a coach mindset:
   - Understands and practices facilitative leadership.
   - Understands Kanban practices and advanced concepts like class of service and improvement models.
   - Has good grip on Kanban metrics – If company's tool of choice fails to provide a metric, Team Coach should be able to work it out using Excel or something else.
2. **Install a physical board:** I would consider it a must have for a co-located team. For a distributed team, a physical board could be considered if majority of the team is in one location. Else, team could project the electronic board on a big TV

screen – in all locations where they have more than 1 member.

3. **Conduct your Daily Connect in Daily Kanban format:** To keep the meeting crisp and effective, it is highly recommended that Teach Coach visits the board about 10 min before the team arrives and identifies work items that need the team's attention.

4. **Keep the items small:** This is applicable for all Agile teams, irrespective of the framework.

   - Most mature Kanban teams either skip estimation or use a short size range (Small/ Medium/ Large or up to 5 points)
   - Encourage 2 or more developers work on larger items (Large or 5 points)

5. **Implement Kanban metrics:** Often ignored by new teams, this is a must-have for any Kanban team. Update metrics regularly and paste them next to the board or in the team area.

6. **Service Delivery Review (Retrospective):** Without this, team could become complacent.

   - Must be done once every 2-4 weeks
   - Team Coach must bring metrics to the room and discuss with the team.

7. **Introduce slack time:** Consider half day slack time once every month for service delivery review plus other activities to be decided by the team. Going home early is not an option.

Mapping Kanban Concepts with Agile Practices

Here is an attempt to map key Kanban concepts/practices with the Agile practices discussed in chapter 4:

Agile Practice	Kanban Concept/Discipline
1. Self-Organizing Teams	
1.1 Visualize work	* Kanban Board * Swim Lanes * Blocker stickies
1.2 Participatory Decision Making	* Change management principles
1.3 Team empowerment	* Team pulls work based on WIP limits
1.4 Team leader as Coach	
1.5 Explicit work discipline	* Make policies explicit
2. Iterative Value Discovery	
2.1 Progressive elaboration	* Discovery/Upstream Kanban * Min-max limits in Discovery Kanban
2.2 Regular Collaboration with Business Stakeholders	* Replenishment Meeting * Dedicated role (SRM) for customer interaction
2.3 Proactive Prioritization	* Discovery Kanban * Class of service

3. Incremental Value Creation	
3.1 Defer Commitment by Limiting Work in Progress	* WIP Limits for - Input queue, Activity columns, Class of service or Swim lanes
3.2 Adaptive planning	* Replenishment meeting * Delivery Planning
3.3 Emergent design	
3.4 Priority-based flow	* Class of service * Swim lanes
3.5 Faster feedback cycles	* WIP limits to control delays * Physical board for cross-team collaboration * Cycle time metrics * Explicit policies for activities
4. Frequent Value Delivery	
4.1 Regular completion of usable features	* Item based flow * Explicit policies * Feature-based swim lanes
4.2 Test automation	
4.3 Regular feedback from stakeholders	
4.4 Automated deployment	
5. Continuous Improvement	
5.1 Daily Connect	* Daily Kanban
5.2 Regular Kaizen events	* Service Delivery Review * Operations Review * Risk Review

APPENDIX

I. Revisiting the Agile Manifesto

In line with Agile mindset, the Agile Manifesto mentioned that 'we are uncovering better ways', suggesting that the Manifesto should change in future based on collective learning of Agile practitioners across the world.

Sadly, that has not happened yet.

Perhaps, a more important question is – does Agile Manifesto need to change?

I believe most of the Agile Manifesto still makes good sense. It does not need an overhaul, but an update to reflect the following concerns would be a welcome step:

- Agile Manifesto was written primarily for software development, but over the past two decades Agile has seen widespread acceptance outside IT industry.
- With waterfall almost faded out, comprehensive documentation is not as big a concern as it was two decades ago.
- There is no explicit value statement on continuous improvement which is the essence of Agile approach.
- The focus on value creation (working software) needs to be widened to focus on end to end value delivery.

Below are my thoughts on how an updated 'industry-neutral' Agile manifesto could look like:

MANIFESTO FOR AGILE SOFTWARE DEVELOPMENT (2.0)

We continue to uncover better ways of developing intelligent solutions through human efforts and have come to value:

1. *Business value delivery* over *Resource utilization*

2. *Team goals* over *Individual goals*

3. *Individuals and interactions* over *Processes and tools*

4. *Responding to change* over *Following a plan*

5. *Continuous improvement* over *a Standardized process*

That is, while there is value in the items on the right, **we value the items on the left more.**

Principles behind the Agile Manifesto

The changes from the original manifesto have been highlighted:

1. Our highest priority is to satisfy the customer through early and **frequent** delivery of **valuable solutions.**
2. Welcome changing requirements, even late in development. Agile processes harness change for the customer's competitive advantage.
3. Deliver working **solution** frequently, within hours, days or weeks rather than once in several months.
4. Business people and **development team** must work together **throughout the value delivery process.**

5. **Develop solutions** around motivated individuals. Give them the environment and support they need and trust them to get the job done.

6. The most efficient and effective method of conveying information to and within a development team is face-to-face conversation.

7. Working **solution** is the primary measure of progress.

8. Agile processes promote sustainable development. The **business people, development team**, and users should be able to maintain a **sustainable pace** indefinitely.

9. Continuous attention to technical excellence and good design enhances agility.

10. Simplicity – **the art of limiting focus on the most essential work right now – is foundational to team effectiveness**.

11. The best architectures, requirements, and designs emerge from self-organizing teams.

12. At regular intervals, the team reflects on how to become more effective, then tunes and adjusts its behaviour accordingly.

While the language of all principles has been left intact, it has been changed for the simplicity principle because most agile practitioners struggle with it.

II.   Estimation Approach in Agile

Key challenges with Time-based Estimation

Let us first understand the key challenges with the traditional approach of estimating work items in time units:

1.   Natural variability in knowledge work

As discussed in Stacey's matrix, knowledge work is not simple work with defined set of steps, repeated over and over again. It involves thinking, analysing and decision making along unchartered paths which makes it difficult to estimate precisely. We need to embrace the inherent variability in effort required to finish knowledge work items.

2.   Variability in People's skills

If you give the user story to 10 developers that have the required technical expertise, the time taken by them to complete the work will be exactly same. Right?

Of course not.

Besides differences in people's skills, people work at different pace and how much time they also might also depend on how lucky they get as knowledge work goes through multiple iterations of trial and error.

3.   Parkinson's Law

Let us take an example to understand this.

Case 1: A developer was given a work item that was estimated to take 5 days. The developer finished it in 7 days.

Case 2: Imagine the same developer and the same work item, if the work item is estimated to take 8 days, how many days do you think the developer would take to finish the work?

I must have posed this question at least 50 times in my trainings and the answer I usually get from participants (mostly team leads speaking from experience) is 8 to 10 days. A small minority thinks the time taken in case 2 will still be 7 days.

Well, this is Parkinson's law. It states that '**work expands to fill the time available**'. In other words, actuals follow the estimates. If something is estimated to take 8 days, actual time will most likely be 8 days or more.

Sad, but true!

There are two common reasons behind Parkinson's law:

i. **Gold Plating or over-processing:** When people have more time than they need for a work item, they tend to do more than needed – trying a new design idea, making the code look perfect, adding extra functionality, coding for future needs, etc.

ii. **Student's Syndrome:** Do you think college students would get higher grades in a 5- or 6-month long semester compared to when the semester is 4-month long?
Probably not. Because most students will study for exams in the last 1-2 weeks only.
Similar things could happen in software development. In case 1, when the estimate was 5 days, the developer might go little easy in the first 3 days, feeling confident all is under control. She begins to feel the urgency to finish on day 4, but realizes there is more than she initially thought and it ends up finishing on day 7.

In case 2, when the estimate is 8 days, the complacency might continue until 5 or 6, pushing the actual effort more than 7 days.

4. Estimating Input or Output?

Many new Agile teams continue their old practice of time-based estimates and define 1 day of effort as 1 story point. Imagine a user story that could be either done by developer X or developer Y. X is an experienced developer and expects to finish the story in 3 days, so she would size it as 3 points. Being a relatively less experienced developer, Y expects to take about 5-6 days for the same story and would like to size it as 5 points.

So, we have one user story that could be sized as 3 points or 5 points depending on who works on it. That is thinking in input terms.

Now, let us think in output terms – how much work is getting done when X works on it vs when Y works on it?

Exactly the same. While input (effort spent) could be different, the output (functionality completed) is same in both cases. So, how much the team has accomplished and how much the client needs to pay should be the same, right? It should be based on output, not input.

Estimating Work Items in Agile

Estimation approach in Agile tries to take care of the four challenges mentioned above. Here are the key elements of the approach:

1. **Estimate size of work (output)**

Agile focuses on estimating the size of work, the amount of work that will be completed, not how much effort (days/hours) would go in. The size is estimated based on three key factors – total amount of work, complexity of work and the associated uncertainty, if any.

2. **Estimate in time-less units**

Since we are measuring output, we measure in time-less unit. This helps in taking the time dimension out and reduces the likelihood of Parkinson's law stretching actual effort.

Three most common scales used are:

    a. Fibonacci series – 1, 2, 3, 5, 8, 13, …
    b. T-shirt sizing – S, M, L, …
    c. Binary – 1, 2, 4, 8, …

Since we measure in timeless units, we need a reference point. It is recommended that we use a medium size work item as a reference and size it as 3 points (or Medium). Other work items are then estimated with this work item as a reference. In the beginning of the project, the reference work item will have an assumed size. As team finishes work items, it is a good idea to pick a recently completed work item as a reference rather than something the team worked on several months back.

3. **Estimate based on team consensus**

To take care of challenge related to differences in people skills, we rely on team consensus for sizing work items. If we were measuring in time units, a consensus would be extremely difficult, and in some cases impossible. Timeless unit combined with the idea of relative sizing of work items help build consensus among team members.

4. Keep the estimation range small

A wide estimation range (say 1 point to 21 points) is more likely to cause confusion among people and lead to inconsistency than a short range of 1 to 5. I have seen mature Scrum teams stay within 5 points range, with 8 points as a rare exception. Please keep in mind 1 point for one team will not be the same as 1 point for another team.

For Kanban teams, I have used 3-point T-shirt sizing (S, M and L) with multiple teams with a simple policy that anything bigger than L must be split into smaller items. If you are using T-shirt sizing, you may want to assign some relative points to S/M/L sizes so the numbers can be added to find team velocity or throughput. Again, it will vary from team to team – it could be 1/2/3, 1/3/5 or 1/2/4. It is best to ask the team, "if Small is 1 point, how big is Medium and Large?"

Estimating Individual Tasks in Agile

Scrum teams usually break down a work item into individual tasks during Sprint planning. Below are quick guidelines estimating tasks:

1. Estimate tasks in hours (max 6-8 hours)

It is okay to estimate tasks in hours as the focus here is to plan team's effort (input) for the Sprint. But, to avoid student's syndrome and maintain a sense of urgency, it is best to keep the tasks small – roughly a day or less (max 6-8 hours), with a possible rare exception to the rule.

II.   Estimation by the assigned individual

To take care of differences in people's skills, the task estimate must be provided by the assigned individual. Hence, it must be done after the task has been pulled by a team member. While team consensus is not required on task estimates, it is okay for team members to seek clarification on each other's estimates as long as it is done in a positive spirit – say, exploring options for a faster/better approach to finish a work item.

III.   What is Scrumban?

Scrumban is a common term in Agile community, shorthand for 'Scrum + Kanban'. A team practising Scrumban adopts practices from both Scrum and Kanban.

Yes, the good news is that Scrum and Kanban can be combined to create possibly a more potent mix, but the sad part is that there is no standard magic formula. I have worked with multiple teams that could claim to be using Scrumban, though no two teams probably have the same process.

Case 1: Scrumban with Sprints

In this case, team primarily uses Scrum (with Sprints), with some elements borrowed from Kanban. Below are some ideas commonly adopted from Kanban (one or more):

i.   **Limit the number of work items in progress:** Instead of starting all committed stories, the team starts no more than 3-4 stories, with team members collaborating on these. Other stories wait until one of the stories in progress gets completed. This helps team start finishing stories faster, plus it helps break the silo culture of 'one developer per story'.

ii. **Physical board with Swim lanes for different types of work:** Common among product development teams that also work on customer issues and production defects (both unplanned work). Teams could also reserve some capacity during Sprint Planning to address unplanned items that might pop up while the Sprint is in progress.

iii. **No breaking of stories into tasks:** Some teams that keep their stories small (effort no more than a few days) stop breaking the story into individual tasks. Their board will also look like a

Kanban board with separate column for testing. They may also switch from task level burndown chart to story-point based burnup chart.

iv. **Flow based Kanban Metrics:** A story pulled into a Sprint is expected to be done within the same Sprint. Unfortunately, it may not be possible always and some teams might experience stories being carried over to the next Sprint on a regular basis. Such teams benefit from tracking cycle time for stories and plotting Kanban metrics like Run Chart and Cycle Time Distribution.

v. **Daily Kanban Format:** Some teams also switch from the common round-robin format for Daily Scrum to Kanban's 'walk the board' format.

Case 2: Scrumban without Sprints

Here teams use Kanban's continuous flow of work and, as a result, it may feel like more of Kanban and less of Scrum. While there is no standard combination here, below are the typical elements that come from Kanban and Scrum.

What comes from Scrum?

- Scrum roles – Product Owner and Scrum Master
- The idea of product backlog and story format, possibly with story point estimation
- Backlog refinement – separate event or part of replenishment meeting
- Daily Scrum format (in combination with Daily Kanban format)
- Sprint Review – once every 2-4 weeks
- Sprint Retrospective – once every 2-4 weeks

What comes from Kanban?

- Continuous flow of work
- Value-stream based visualization of work
- WIP limits at activity level or for the entire workflow
- Kanban's flow-based metrics
- Weekly replenishment meeting (replaces Sprint Planning)
- Daily Kanban format
- Service Delivery Review (elements merged with Retrospective format)

IV. Mapping XP Concepts with key Agile Practices

In late 1990's and early 2000's, Extreme Programming (XP) was gaining good popularity. Some say it was more popular than Scrum. But somehow, over the past two decades, XP has lost out as a project execution approach. I see three possible reasons for this. First, XP is rigorous discipline; it requires a huge shift in how teams do things. Not everyone's cup of tea. Second, Scrum has a significant overlap with XP (e.g., iteration-based planning), making Scrum look like an easier option than XP. Third, Scrum Alliance has done an amazing job in marketing Scrum.

The result, today what is left of XP is just the technical practices – TDD (test-driven development), CI (continuous integration), etc. The process part (iterations, stories, etc.) has been replaced by Scrum. The table below gives a quick summary of how the original XP concepts map to our key Agile practices. It is highly recommended that you explore Extreme Programming on your own.

Agile Practice	XP Concept/Discipline
1. Self-Organizing Teams	
1.1 Visualize work	* Task Board
1.2 Participatory Decision Making	* Planning Game * Whole team
1.3 Team empowerment	* Collective code ownership * Sustainable pace
1.4 Team leader as Coach	
1.5 Explicit work discipline	* Code standards

2. Iterative Value Discovery	
2.1 Progressive elaboration	* User Story to capture requirements
2.2 Regular Collaboration with Business Stakeholders	* On-site customer
2.3 Priority-based flow	
3. Incremental Value Creation	
3.1 Defer Commitment by Limiting Work in Progress	* Small releases * Limited scope for an Iteration
3.2 Adaptive planning	* Planning games
3.3 Emergent design	* Simple design * Refactoring
3.4 Priority-based flow	* Iteration
3.5 Faster feedback cycles	* Test-Driven development * Continuous Integration * Pair programming
4. Frequent Value Delivery	
4.1 Regular completion of usable features	* Small value-driven stories * Small releases
4.2 Test automation	* Test-Driven development * Continuous Integration
4.3 Regular feedback from stakeholders	* On-site customer * Customer tests
4.4 Automated deployment	
5. Continuous Improvement	
5.1 Daily Connect	* Daily Standup
5.2 Regular Kaizen events	* Code refactoring

V.   A Short Note on Scaling Agile

Scaling Agile means spreading Agile beyond a single team of 10 (or less) people, and has two different dimensions:

i.   Adopting Agile across the entire organization

For scaling Agile across the wider organization, we need to look at each team separately. If the teams are small (up to 10 members) and independent, adopting Agile would be their independent journey – each team may independently choose Scrum, Kanban, a combination or some other Agile approach depending upon what suits them best.

You may NOT need a Scaling framework like SAFe, LeSS, Nexus or Scrum@Scale here. *Those are meant for multiple inter-dependent teams (next point).*

ii.   Adopting Agile for large programs that may have multiple tightly inter-dependent teams (total 50+ people)

You might need a scaling framework here if you have multiple teams with high degree of inter-dependencies – a single product, common code base and a common release.

Let me stress an important point again – if you have multiple teams in a business unit working on independent products, projects or deliverables (with minimal dependencies), you do not need a scaling framework. Each team needs to adopt Agile independently, of course, with some common organization support. A grand Scaled Agile solution might sound very smart or fancy, but will possibly waste too much of your time, money and energy for no real benefit.

A scaling framework does not change the core of Agile at team level; it primarily provides a structure and process for multiple teams to coordinate their efforts. Since the focus of scaling is coordination, the cadence of team meetings may be impacted, but the everyday Agile practices at team level (Scrum, Kanban, etc.) will continue to be just the same.

Here are some additional considerations before you adopt a scaled Agile solution (SAFe, LeSS, Nexus, etc.):

1. Allow teams to practice Agile at team level for 6 months or more, until they have familiarized themselves with new ways of working and gained some agile maturity.

2. Mentor and coach your team leads so they have embraced the idea of empiricism and self-organizing teams.

3. Ensure the initial resistance to Agile has subsided significantly before you start your efforts to scale Agile.

4. For small programs with up to 5 teams (40-50 people), a grand solution like SAFe or LeSS may prove to be expensive over-engineering. You may explore some simple scaling options like Scrum of Scrums or Kanban Method. Or, you may choose to scale Agile organically – facilitate discussion among team leads and team members on how teams must improve their coordination with each other, followed by regular inspect and adapt cycles.

Further Reading

1. *'The Scrum Guide', 2017, by Ken Schwaber and Jeff Sutherland.*
A short book (less than 20 pages) that provides a crisp introduction on Scrum. A must read for every Scrum practitioner and the starting point for learning Scrum.

2. *'Succeeding with Agile', 2010, Mike Cohn.*
A detailed introduction of Agile and Scrum, it covers various dimensions of agile adoption, but focuses primarily on Scrum.

3. *'Kanban: Successful Evolutionary Change for Technology Organizations', 2010, David J. Anderson.*
This book provides a detailed introduction to Kanban Method, with lots of examples and case studies. Since the body of knowledge on Kanban Method has evolved significantly in last 5-7 years, a new version of this book is very much needed.

4. *'Kanban from the Inside', 2014, Michael Burrows.*
Mike builds on the concepts provided in David's book and shares a step by step approach (STATIK) for introducing Kanban to a new team. His STATIK approach is widely popular in Kanban community.

5. *'Coaching Agile Teams', 2010, Lyssa Adkins.*
This book provides a comprehensive guidance on how to coach Agile teams. A must read for Agile Coaches, Scrum Masters and senior managers leading multiple Agile teams.

6. *'Five Dysfunctions of a Team', 2005, Patrick Lencioni.*
A book written in the form of a story (fiction) explaining five common dysfunctions that prevent teams from achieving

high performance. Highly recommended read book for Scrum Masters and Agile Coaches.

7. *http://mountaingoatsoftware.com, a site owned by Mike Cohn*
    Mike has good amount of knowledge available on his website in the form of blogs and videos - blogs are free but videos are mostly available through chargeable online learning programs.

8. *http://HowtoAgile.com, a site owned and maintained by Sanjay (author of this book)*
    This site has blogs on various topics related to Agile, Scrum, Kanban and Agile Coaching.

About the Author

Sanjay Kumar is an independent Agile Coach and Trainer, with over 20 years of IT experience. Sanjay specializes in introducing agile in an evolutionary/low-impact manner that aims to bring quick results while maintaining high motivation and low resistance. He has helped start-ups, mid-size organizations and big corporates embrace Agile ways of working.

As an Agile Trainer, Sanjay has delivered more than a hundred public and corporate training session on Agile, Scrum, Kanban, Facilitation and Coaching skills. Prior to his current role as an Agile Coach and Trainer, Sanjay spent over fifteen years in developing and delivering software solutions for different domains such as finance, healthcare, retail and shipping; and has worked in a variety of work environments – from start-ups to big corporates.

You may learn more about Sanjay through his website http://HowtoAgile.com or his LinkedIn profile http://linkedin.com/in/sunjaykumar. You may share your feedback on this book or contact him for your organization's training/coaching needs via email sanjay@howtoagile.com.

Manufactured by Amazon.ca
Bolton, ON

12816516R00066